Ryūkyū Kempo
History & Practice

Master's Edition

Kubichiridushi

RYŪKYŪ KEMPO: MASTER'S EDITION
Copyright © 2018 by *Kubichiridushi*
—Fifth Edition—
ISBN-10: 0998065439
ISBN-13: 978-0998065434

All rights reserved. No part of this book may be reproduced in any form without prior, written permission from the publisher or author, except in the case of brief quotations in articles or reviews.

The material in this book is intended for educational purposes only. No one should undertake the practice of self-defense or healing without qualified instruction and supervision, and an awareness of the criminal and civil limitations on the use of force in self-defense and the practice of medicine. Physical combat is an inherently dangerous activity. Medical diagnosis and treatment should be provided by qualified healthcare professionals. The author, publisher, and distributors are not responsible in any manner for any injury or liability that may result from practicing—or attempting to practice—the techniques described herein. Any application of the information contained in this work is at the reader's sole and exclusive risk. Because of the danger of injury to oneself and others, prior to engaging in any type of self-defense program it is advisable to consult both a professional martial arts instructor and a licensed physician.

This book was printed in the United States of America by Stirling Bridge Publications; a publisher specializing in works dedicated to exploring the power of one.

stirlingbridge@mail.com

For Grandmaster George Dillman

Your dedication to the arts,
your ability to bring people together,
and your Promethean efforts
to illuminate the darkness
have changed the martial
landscape forever...

From a grateful generation

CONTENTS

	Foreword	1
1.	The Art	8
2.	The Man	11
3.	*Kihon*	24
4.	*Kata*	28
5.	*Kumite*	35
6.	*Kobudo*	38
7.	*Kyusho-jitsu*	43
8.	The Rubicon	48
9.	The Looking Glass	51
10.	Angle & Direction	53
11.	Polarity & Quadrant	55
12.	Breathing	58
13.	Sound	60

Ryūkyū Kempo

14. Stance	63
15. Color	65
16. Extremities	67
17. Placement	69
18. Emotion	71
19. Tool Selection	73
20. Auras	75
21. *Lo Shu*	77
22. The Source	79
23. Humanity	85
24. The Camp	88
25. The Science	91
26. **The Master Class**	101
27. The Next Generation	151
28. Act of Succession	199
Epilogue	202

FOREWORD:
Chris Thomas

If you are reading this book, you likely already know who George Dillman is. But, on the off-chance that this book is your introduction to him, then know that he is one of the most recognizable martial arts teachers in the world. He is a renowned expert in *kyusho-jitsu*, or pressure point fighting, and, since about 1985, he has traveled the world teaching martial artists how to incapacitate an opponent with little effort by touching and hitting nerves and acupuncture points.

The methods of *kyusho-jitsu* were once secret teaching, so virtually no martial artists alive knew the methods. If Einstein was right, and "fortune favors the prepared mind," then fortune favored George Dillman who found himself in the right places at the right times to learn these methods. And, as a result, what was once secret teaching is now an accessible skill for the dedicated martial arts practitioner.

Ryūkyū Kempo

One would think that this would be viewed as a positive thing in the martial arts community. However, for as long as I have known George Dillman, there has been controversy around him. These controversies generally fall into two categories: criticism of the teaching, and criticism of the man.

Early on, criticism of the teaching, of pressure point methods, abounded. Some said that pressure points weren't real; they were simply chop-sockey mythology. Others argued that pressure points were too dangerous to teach openly. For the most part, these two criticism have disappeared, falling victim to the fact that:

(1) George Dillman has knocked out so many people; and

(2) They are still alive to talk about it.

Later, the criticism changed to, "Sure, pressure points work in the school or the demonstration, but not in a real fight." But even this has lost conviction, as more and more practitioners of pressure point fighting survive real-world encounters using those skills. And, people see pressure points in "real" fights all the time. Even the casual viewer of MMA has seen light-strike knock outs in the ring when a punch lands "right on the button." Pressure point practitioners can describe and demonstrate those "buttons" at any time. (Though, MMA also shows that the well-rounded martial artist has more in the toolbox.)

In the late 90s, Bob "Pit Bull" Golden, a student of Dillman's, demonstrated a knock out with virtually no physical contact. This began an exploration among the Dillman group of the old method of *toate-jitsu*, or "no touch" knock out (*Toate-jitsu* literally means "distance [*to*] hit [*ate*] fighting method [*jitsu*]"). In Chinese martial arts, especially *i-chuan*, it is called *ling kong jing*, which is usually translated "empty force"). But, since the idea of a knock out performed without physical contact flies in the face of accepted expectation, the debunkers, doubters and deniers were (and still are) out in force. In response, I will only repeat here what I have said elsewhere:

For a debunker to prove that a no-touch knock out is impossible, they must prove that it can never be done. On the other hand, for us to prove *toate-jitsu* is possible, we only have to do it once, and reproduce it a second time. Since we have already accomplished this, the real questions are, "What is the mechanism (or mechanisms) behind the phenomenon?" And, "What are the practical values and limitations of the method?"

In many ways, criticism of George Dillman the man is more intense than the criticism of the methods. I think this is because discrediting Dillman is a simple way for people to avoid admitting their own ignorance. But, since these criticisms have continued, they are worth a mention here. One of the most common early criticisms of Dillman was, "He's just out to make a buck." Maybe. But, how else would I have even been exposed to this material if he hadn't made it available for purchase? And it requires something of a true salesman to spread and propagate a radical re-thinking of entrenched martial arts dogma. Who else would have made this information known, if not Dillman?

Another attack on the man has been, "He just stole Oyata's techniques." Sorry, but I need to give you a little history, here: Taika Oyata (a.k.a. Seiyu Oyata) is a master of Okinawan martial arts. Oyata-sensei trained under Shigeru Nakamura, and was deeply involved with Nakamura's Okinawan Kempo League. He also received training in *ti* (a precursor art to *karate*) at the beginning of his martial career, and, was somehow involved with the late Sekichi Uehara of Motobu-ryu Udante (Motobu-ryu is a classical system of *ti* taught for generations within the important Motobu family).

In the years following the death of Nakamurua-sensei (Januray, 1969), there was conflict among the members of the Okinawan Kempo League, with the result that Oyata left Okinawa for the U.S. (where he already had students and a fledging organization) and disassociated himself from the Okinawan Kempo League. Because he was no longer affiliated with the Okinawan Kempo League, he began to call his art Ryūkyū Kempo; a generic term for Okinawan karate which has been in use from at least the 19th century (and, it is also another way of saying Okinawan Kempo).

So, back to the criticism of Dillman, that, "He just stole Oyata's techniques." Sensei Dillman had a brief, but very significant, encounter with Okinawan karate master Hohan Soken in 1972. Soken was the direct successor of Bushi Matsumura, a 19th century teacher who in many ways defined the shape of all karate to follow. Soken took a liking to Dillman (telling others that Dillman had a good aura). Soken gave Dillman an impromptu private lesson, and included Dillman in a small and select group who received a set of pressure point notes and charts. It is an important truth that life-changing ideas take a while to sink in. Dillman admitted to me that he didn't really understand what Soken had shown him, and that he had filed away the notes he received from Soken.

Ryūkyū Kempo

In the early 80's, Dillman became a student of Oyata. He sponsored seminars with Oyata, had Oyata at his dojo, hosted Oyata in his home, and stayed at Oyata's house. In fact, in December of 1983, Dillman and second wife Kim were stranded by a huge snowstorm in Oyata's home for ten days. Dillman received the rank of nana-dan (7th dan, dated October 23, 1983) from Oyata, and appeared with Oyata on the cover of Official Karate Magazine (July, 1984). So, how can Dillman have "stolen" Oyata's techniques if Oyata taught him without reservation? And Dillman has always given Oyata credit, often stopping in the middle of teaching a seminar to say, "I learned this technique from Oyata."

Now, it is true that Oyata and Dillman had a falling out. Dillman doesn't like to talk about it, and when he finally told me the story (after I had known him for years!), I was surprised by the deep emotion and loss he expressed. Second wife Kim, was also present for the argument. After their divorce, and after both George Dillman and Kim Dillman had remarried (Suzie, and Skip, respectively), I obtained an independent account from Kim so that I could corroborate what George had told me.

To understand what happened, we must return to the time when the Dillmans were snowed in at Oyata's home. Dillman told me that he had been allowed to use Oyata's private bathroom (the other bathroom in Oyata's home being occupied). As he passed through Oyata's bedroom he saw, on Oyata's desk, a set of pressure point charts. Instantly things fell into place. He realized that Oyata's notes looked like the ones from Soken (except, in Japanese). And Dillman realized that this was what had led him to Oyata in the first place. And this also explained how Dillman was able to progress quickly as one of Oyata's students, being graded higher than others who had been with Oyata longer.

The falling out happened after a seminar in March, 1984. Oyata was at George and Kim Dillman's home, Oyata was drinking Wild Turkey, and George had had some beers. At one point, Kim was in the kitchen, and George asked her if she thought he should show Oyata the pressure point charts and notes he had received from Hohan Soken. Kim told George that she didn't think this was a good idea. But, as those of us who know George Dillman well can attest, he is a bit stubborn when he gets an idea in his head. So, he went, got the notes from the filing cabinet, brought them out, and showed them to Oyata. What follows is from Kim's written account.

Oyata looked at the notes, then at George. He got up, threw the notes onto the coffee table and said, "You no need sensei." With that he walked to his room... Shortly afterwards, Oyata came back out of his room... I saw the look on Oyata's face when he came out of his room, and it was very dark and angry... I heard Oyata say, "You no need sensei, you have all points." George replied, "That's not true, sensei. I have the papers, but you showed me how to make this work. Thank you."

After that, things went from bad to worse. Without realizing it, or even realizing how, George Dillman had committed a serious cultural offense. In U.S. society, a student pleases the teacher by doing extra-credit work, studying material not included in the syllabus, and reading ahead. But, in the classical culture of Okinawan and Japanese martial arts, the student entrusts himself or herself entirely to the master's leading. To "read ahead" or study outside the syllabus is like a slap in the face; a vote of "no confidence" in the master's skill and wisdom in the molding of the student. The next morning Oyata left the Dillman home without saying a word, their relationship irrevocably damaged.

About four months later, Dillman and his students attended Oyata-sensei's summer camp. Oyata was cordial, but there was an awkwardness between them. Unfortunately, it soon became apparent that Dillman had committed another cultural sin. As a traditional Okinawan teacher, Oyata routinely held back essential information from his students, or taught them techniques in an intentionally misleading manner. This practice was all part of the customary manner in which the arts had been taught in the past. Students were treated like outsiders, and kept from knowing much until they were deemed worthy.

But George Dillman, with an American sensibility about the loyalty a teacher owes the student, treated everybody like insiders. And so, things which Oyata had withheld from all but his inner circle, Dillman shared openly with his own students. And when the direct students of Oyata, and Dillman's students were talking on Saturday evening, Oyata's students were dismayed to hear about the knowledge which Dillman's group all seemed to possess. And this created rivalry and conflict.

At the end of the weekend, as Dillman was preparing to leave in his motor home, Oyata came over. He criticized Dillman's students for talking too much and causing problems, and implied that Dillman ought not teach so freely. Then, he showed Dillman a couple more pressure points, and said goodbye. The real issues between them remained unaddressed. But how could they resolve their argument when each one was in the right from his own culture's perspective? So, like friends who simply stop calling each other, Dillman and Oyata parted ways. Yet, despite this ending, Dillman has honored his former teacher, making Oyata's name and techniques known to countless thousands around the world.

And, there has been a positive as well—ask almost anyone with a knowledge of martial arts to name a student of Oyata, and they will name Dillman. Ask them to name another student of Oyata and they will draw a blank. And I believe the reason is fairly simple: students with continuing access to Oyata waited for him to teach them. Dillman, estranged from Oyata, used everything Oyata taught him to develop into his own martial artist. Dillman has not tried to merely reproduce Oyata's techniques—to become an Oyata clone—so much as understand the underlying principles. And understanding those underlying principles has enabled Dillman to apply them, literally turning the collection of techniques he learned from Oyata into a virtually limitless curriculum (I have never seen him run out of something to teach, because he can develop brilliant techniques on the spot).

Of course, some may say that the reason Dillman is the only recognizable name among Oyata's students is that Dillman knows how to market himself. But the last fifty years of martial arts in America has been littered with self-promoters. Yet, only a handful of martial artists have actually changed the culture and practice of martial arts. My list would include: Bruce Lee, Ed Parker, Wally Jay, Remy Presas, the Gracie family, perhaps two or three others, and George Dillman. As martial arts historian Patrick McCarthy (himself no fan of Dillman) admits, "George Dillman has forced a generation of martial artists to rethink their kata."

So, there has always been controversy about George Dillman, but I don't get it.

George Dillman is supposed to be a big ego. If that's so, why does he turn over portions of his seminars to senior students to teach, and include opportunities for anyone of any rank or affiliation to get up and demonstrate a technique?

George Dillman is supposed to be about self-promotion. If that's so, why does he let his students sell their own instructional videos at his seminars, and why does he encourage them to teach seminars of their own around the world?

George Dillman is supposed to be a huckster. If that's so, why does he challenge everyone to study and research to see if the things he teaches are correct?

George Dillman is supposed to be a sham. If that's so, why is there such a long list of those who have become believers because they have experienced the techniques?

I was changing after a seminar one weekend, and I overheard an interesting comment. The speaker had trained in a few different arts, including a Ryūkyū Kempo off-shoot (apparently under some other former student of Oyata). I heard him say, "I expected Dillman to be able to do it; but I didn't expect all his people to be able to do it, too." And this, ultimately, is the answer to any and all critics of George Dillman—his people can do it, too.

I have, for a long time, been a business partner with George Dillman in the production and publication of books on pressure point fighting, so I know how honest and savvy he is.

I have, for a long time, been a friend of George Dillman, so I know how interesting and funny he is.

I have, for a long time, been a confidante of George Dillman, so I know how generous and vulnerable his heart is.

But, all of these things have become true, first and foremost, because I have, for a long time, been a student of George Dillman. And, as his student I have found him to be open in his teaching, eager to share all he knows, and glad to have his students discover new things so that he might learn from them.

And because of George Dillman, *I can do it too...*

—Chris Thomas

Ryūkyū Kempo

CHAPTER ONE:
The Art

◆ **Kempo** (sometimes rendered Ke<u>n</u>po) is the Japanese translation of the Chinese term: *quán fǎ*—the way of the fist.

Over time, this word has been used to describe many different martial arts systems, including:

1. Shorinji Kempo: A discipline that sprang from Shaolin Kung Fu in the 1940s;

2. American Kenpo: A style founded by Ed Parker in the 1950s;

3. Okinawan Kempo: An ancient fighting method indigenous to the people inhabiting the island of Okinawa and its environs.

◆ **Ryūkyū** refers to a chain of islands—the largest of which is Okinawa—that stretch, like stepping stones, in an arc across the South China Sea, from Taiwan to Kyushu, with China to the West, Japan and Korea to the North, and the Philippines to the South.

◆ **Ryūkyū Kempo**, then, is the martial art that evolved over centuries in this focal archipelago.

Many traditional karate systems from this region of the world are based on three primary fields of study: *kihon, kata,* and *kumite*. To these, Ryūkyū Kempo adds two more: *kobudo* and *kyusho-jitsu*.

> **Kihon:** Basic techniques
> **Kata:** Forms
> **Kumite:** Free Fighting
> **Kobudo:** Weapons
> **Kyusho-jitsu:** Pressure Point Fighting

As a result, an experienced practitioner of this art is truly armed at all points.

> The total warrior is truly armed at all points.
> —The Master

Ryūkyū Kempo

CHAPTER TWO:
The Man

Whether or not they agree with his methods, most martial arts commentators acknowledge that the man most responsible for disseminating the art of Ryūkyū Kempo throughout the world in the Twentieth century and beyond is George Dillman.

Born in Philadelphia, Pennsylvania, on November 23, 1942, of Irish, German, and Italian ancestry, George Anthony Dillman III likes to joke that his ethnic ancestors were known for two things: drinking and brawling, so he was destined to be a fighter.

Dillman's stepfather—Chester L. Mengle—was the first Command Sergeant Major in the U.S. armed forces and taught self-defense to soldiers during the Second World War. Dillman attributes much of his interest in the military and the martial arts to the influence of his stepfather, who taught him some of the rudiments of self-defense as a child, including punches, kicks, and the use of pepper powder.

At the age of nine Dillman enrolled in a judo class at the local YMCA. He studied this art for several years, learning the basic hip throws, foot sweeps and other types of takedowns, until the instructor eventually moved away. In his early teens, Dillman moved out of his mother's house and got his own apartment, supporting himself, at least in part, by fighting for boxing purses.

> During those early years I boxed on the F.O.B. Circuit (Friends of Boxing) out of the Pottsville Area YMCA. Charles Meagher was the physical director. Tony Super was my coach and manager. Les Carrell was the organizer. We fought at armories in Scranton, Wilkes-Barre, Altoona and at least one time down in Philadelphia. They were known as "smokers" because everyone was drinking and smoking and calling you names. I had a tough time dealing with all that, but I fought to make money. We were paid three dollars a round, five if we won and twenty for the knockout. I used to sit around in the locker room afterwards and look at the element I was in and think, "this ain't for me, I've got to get out of this." My record was 25-3 when I finished. I fought twice more in the military and won representing our barracks, so my overall boxing record would be 27-3.
>
> —Grandmaster George Dillman (GMGD)

After graduating from high school in 1961, Dillman enlisted in the Army. His basic training took place at Fort Knox, Kentucky, where he met a fellow soldier who practiced karate.

A quick demonstration of the power of the art made a believer out of Dillman and he joined a nearby dojo that same evening.

Following his assignment to a post in Harrisburg, Pennsylvania, Dillman met Harry Smith, the Sixth Dan student of Isshin Ryu founder Tatsuo Shimabuku, and began training with the martial arts legend. He remembers this as "the roughest thing I'd ever seen… he started out with a hundred people and soon he's down to twenty-five, but they were tough as nails." Among the many lessons Dillman learned from this art was the importance of breathing.

> What impressed me the most in Isshin Ryu was the breathing, and I've kept it in my system to this day. Harry explained that fighting is like swimming. Once you get out there you either sink or you swim. And breathing should be thought of like fighting underwater. If you take a breath at the wrong time, you die. In a fight, if you take a breath at the wrong time, you die. The first four forms were created to teach you breath control. Other styles don't have that and you will be able to defeat them because of it.
>
> —GMGD

In 1963, Dillman was commissioned as an officer and reassigned to Washington DC.

It was here that he began formally teaching karate classes. At this duty station he also met another soldier who had done a tour of duty in Okinawa and was studying Tae Kwon Do at Jhoon Rhee's school. The two worked out together regularly, and it was in this context that Dillman developed his high kicking skills and flexibility for which he is so well known.

In 1965, Dillman met and began training with Daniel Pai. Dillman credits Pai with teaching him the importance of flowing technique and introducing him to the idea of pressure points.

Pai then introduced Dillman to Ed Parker and Bruce Lee the following year, resulting in the three visiting and exchanging ideas with one another on occasion over the years that followed. From Parker, Dillman learned the value of natural movements, like the parallel upper block, and the three-quarter punch. From observing Lee, he came to appreciate the power of relaxation—and even humor—in martial arts training. It was also Lee who first identified the connection between acupuncture and pressure points.

Ryūkyū Kempo

By 1967, Dillman was entering—and winning—tournaments all over the United States. With over three hundred awards to his name during his nine year competitive career, *Official Karate* magazine would go on to describe him as, "one of the winningest competitors karate has ever known." He was four-times National Karate Champion (1969-1972), and was consistently ranked among the top ten competitors in the nation in almost every category during this timeframe.

In 1970, in recognition of his expertise with a number of different, traditional, Okinawan weapons, Masanao Takazawa awarded Dillman his Fifth Dan in kobudo.

In 1972, Dillman ran into Muhammad Ali at a diner in Reading. It was in fact the second time their paths had crossed, the first being a sports banquet at the hotel New Yorker five years earlier. On this occasion, however, Ali was in Pennsylvania to set up a training camp, and Dillman quickly became a member of the Champ's team, making him the only person to have trained with both Bruce Lee and Muhammad Ali, and many boxing aficionados claim that the effects of his association with the karate master could also be seen in Ali's fighting style over the years that followed.

Ryūkyū Kempo

In this same year, Dillman met and trained with Hohan Soken, an Okinawan karate master who was attending an event in the United States. At this gathering, Dillman performed a kata. When he had finished, Soken approached him and said, "it hurts me here [indicating his heart] to see you do such fine kata and not know why you do it." Soken then explained that when the Okinawan masters first trained American soldiers, they often had neither the time nor the inclination to convey the deep meaning of the techniques; a failing that he now wanted to help address. As a result, Soken made a rough drawing of the human body and marked the pressure points, explaining that these targets, and their corresponding striking methods, were contained in the kata. He also shared a set of notes describing these methods with some of the senior practitioners in attendance. As a result, after years of focusing on *kihon, kata, kumite,* and *kobudo,* Dillman began to appreciate the pivotal importance of *kyusho-jitsu* to the well-rounded martial artist.

Hohan Soken died in 1982. In 1983 Dillman first met Seiyu Oyata at a seminar in Missouri. This event opened with a series of pressure point knockouts, and Dillman instantly recognized Oyata's techniques to be applications of Hohan Soken's teachings. Over the years that followed, Dillman visited and trained regularly with Oyata, and was promoted by him to the rank of Seventh Dan. Sadly, the two masters eventually clashed over administrative matters and went their separate ways, but out of respect for Oyata, Dillman adopted the name Ryūkyū Kempo, and continues to employ a patch with kanji written by Oyata to this day.

> We ended up parting ways, but I like to think we still remained friends on our parting. One of the first things Oyata told me was, "you shouldn't say Okinawan Kempo, because Okinawa is one place, and there are a chain of islands where that art came from. Your art should be called Ryūkyū Kempo." To this day I've taken his advice and kept that name. And to this day my students wear the patch with his handwriting for: "Ryūkyū Kempo."
>
> —GMGD

Finding himself without a teacher, Dillman sought out and partnered with some of the most well-known and highly-respected headmasters in the United States at that time: Professor Wally Jay, the Founder of Small Circle Jujitsu; Professor Remy Presas, the Founder of Modern Arnis; and Grandmaster Leo Fong, the Founder of Wei Kuen Do.

For almost twenty years, these world-class martial artists traveled the world in various combinations, conducting seminars at which they shared venues, concepts, and students, and a generation of martial artists whose certificates bear all their signatures is richer for it. It is this council of elders who ultimately promoted Dillman to Tenth Dan and acknowledged him as the head of his own system.

In 1984, Dillman began an in-depth study of the human nervous system with the assistance of one of his students—Dr. Ralph Buschbacher—who was a medical student with access to the cadaver laboratory and staff expertise at the University of Virginia at that time.

In 1988, Dillman traveled to Japan, where he taught seminars in Tokyo and Osaka. During this trip, he also obtained and studied a copy of a pressure point study conducted over thirty-five years (from 1935-1970).

In 1992, *Black Belt* magazine named Dillman as its Instructor of the Year (he was often featured in this publication both before and afterwards, including on the cover of the January 1990 issue).

Ryūkyū Kempo

In 1997, Muhammad Ali sold his training camp in Pennsylvania to Dillman at a deep discount, in honor of its initial purpose and subsequent owner. For the next two decades, this idyllic retreat served as the home base for a cadre of Ryūkyū Kempo practitioners from all around the world.

In 2006, Dillman and a contingent of his students traveled to China, to visit and train at, among other places, the Shaolin Temple and Tongren Hospital in Beijing.

And he has plans to make a pilgrimage to Okinawa—the birthplace of the art he loves so much—in the not-too-distant future.

In recent years Dillman has promoted a number of his most senior students to Tenth Dan, and has increasingly allowed them to take on the lion's share of the teaching responsibilities.

> He who brings even one good student to the path has repaid his debt to past masters. The enlightened teacher strives to make himself redundant.
> —The Master

In 2016, the Camp that had come to be both a sanctuary and a fountainhead for a generation of martial artists, was finally sold, marking the end of an era.

Ryūkyū Kempo

CHAPTER THREE:
Kihon

At their core, the martial arts are about the ability to prevail in combat. As anyone who has faced an opponent inside or outside the ring knows full well, the techniques that carry the day in this context are generally not the advanced moves, but rather, the fundamentals.

In order to be of maximum operational value, a technique must be automatic, adaptable, and absolute.

1. Automatic: It is not enough that the practitioner understands conceptually how a particular move works. Rather, it must have been practiced so many times that its performance is immediate, instinctive, and flawless. If it hasn't been practiced at least ten thousand times, it probably isn't ready for use in earnest;

2. Adaptable: No two engagements are the exactly same. As a result, attempting a technique that only works on *some* people or in *some* situations can be quite dangerous. For this reason, it is important not only to practice with live partners, but with partners of all different shapes and sizes, in order to ensure that the weapon in question works against a wide variety of targets.

3. Absolute: When employed, the technique should be a decisive fight-ender. It must be reliable enough that it can be counted on to do the job, every time. And while raw power is only one of several necessary ingredients for such a technique, it is worth considering the following rule of thumb in this regard: If the weapon isn't strong enough to break a one inch pine board, it's probably not ready for inclusion in your martial armamentarium.

CUT DOWN!

There is an apocryphal tale in the Japanese martial tradition of a merchant who inadvertently gave offense to a samurai and was duly challenged to a duel to the death the next morning. Knowing nothing of the sword arts, he approached a master instructor and asked if there was anything he could learn in the short time remaining that could possibly help him prevail. "Yes," the master replied: "cut down!"

In keeping with these principles, a few, strong, simple, familiar tools will generally be sufficient to perform most tasks:

- **Parry:** A fundamental tenet of Ryūkyū Kempo is that the wide, arcing, closed-fist techniques commonly taught as karate blocks are in fact something else altogether, and are not intended to sweep aside an attacking limb as common understanding suggests.

KIHON, BUNKAI, TUITE, AND KYUSHO

Two notable examples of this fallacy—or rather, enigma—are the 'double block' and the 'augmented block'. When the eastern arts first began to wend their way into western training halls, the 'double block' was often taught as a way of defending against two simultaneous strikes, and the 'augmented block' was explained as a way of reinforcing the basic side block. Even a rudimentary understanding of the realities of free-fighting, however, reveals that neither of these would be particularly efficient ways of warding off the putative attacks. Why, then, did the past masters include them in the syllabus of basic techniques *(kihon)*?

Ryūkyū Kempo

> Ryūkyū Kempo's compelling answer is that when properly decoded, these familiar fundamentals have highly efficient and effective applications *(bunkai)*. The movement of the 'double block,' for example, describes exactly the motion required to execute a figure four arm lock or break *(tuite jutsu)*, while the position, angle, and direction of the 'augmented block' clearly indicates SI-8—a *he-sea* point known as *Xiaohai*: 'the small sea'— more commonly known in the western world as the 'funny bone' point *(kyusho-jitsu)*.

The defensive technique of choice, rather, is a short, sharp, direct, open-handed deflection known as a parry, which is more agile, effective, and sensitive than a traditional block.

This can be performed either single or double-handed (as in the case of a 'windmill block'), and the hand-weapon used to accomplish this move— the *shuto* or willow-leaf palm—can also be used to hammer, slice, spear, and cup.

◆ **Punch:** Primarily intended for use against a soft target, the Ryūkyū Kempo three-quarter turn punch is anatomically stronger, physically more effective, and energetically superior to many other forms of closed-fist striking. This hand-weapon can be applied in a variety of ways. Jabs, crosses, hooks, and uppercuts, for example, comprise the entirety of western boxing's armamentarium, to which such arts as Leo Fong's *Wei Kuen Do* add variations like the hammer fist, axe fist, and back fist.

- **Palm Heel:** Primarily intended for use against a hard target, the palm heel allows the practitioner to deliver a solid blow with the hand without risking injury to the delicate knuckles or fingers. While this hand-weapon employs the palm, its configuration is slightly different from the shuto/willow-leaf palm described above.

- **Front Kick:** Usually delivered with the ball of the foot, a front kick need be neither high nor tremendously powerful to reposition the opponent, throw him off balance, or inflict injury. A common target for this technique is the stomach or pelvis.

- **Side Kick:** Usually delivered with the knife edge of the foot, a side kick can do tremendous damage when applied to the opponent's knee at the correct angle. This technique is the quintessential fight-ender.

- **Roundhouse Kick:** Usually delivered with the instep, the roundhouse kick can do significant damage as well, but is often better employed as a distracting, distancing, or 'whittling' technique, as is frequently the case in Muay Thai matches.

These six techniques alone, if practiced and performed properly, are perfectly capable of delivering decisive victories both within and outside the ring.

> Beware the man of one book.
> —The Master

There are, however, many more, the regular practice of which will train the body over time to perform the movements needed to prevail in combat:

- Horse Stance
- Front Stance
- Side Stance
- Cat Stance
- Back Stance
- Cross Stance
- Back Kick
- Stepover Kick
- Diagonal Kick

- Side Block
- Upper Block
- Down Block
- Inside Block
- Double Block
- Augment Block
- Shuto Block
- X- Block
- Wedge Block

- Knife Hand
- Ridge Hand
- Spear Hand
- Wrist Strike
- Elbow Strike
- Backhand Strike
- Finger Strike
- Knuckle Strike
- Raking Strike

Ryūkyū Kempo

CHAPTER FOUR:
Kata

Kata—also known as forms or patterns—are veritable encyclopedias of fighting techniques. When practiced correctly, each move has at least one, clearly-decipherable, highly-effective, real-world, application. Learning and performing kata in this manner is vastly slower than simply memorizing a sequence of movements, but is this very **understanding** that marks the difference between kata and mere dance.

While experienced teachers afford students wide latitude in deciphering the meaning of any given move, there are certain core requirements for a valid interpretation:

1. Resemblance: Subject to certain obvious limitations, the interpretation should at least resemble the movement in the form from which it is drawn. Past masters encoded these techniques into the ancient patterns for a reason, so, while a certain amount of poetic license may be required in representing the position of the opponent, or the execution of the move, it makes little sense to strain the connection between the representation and the interpretation to the breaking point. When the student first learns the proper application of a given part of a form, he will recognize its propriety immediately and instinctively;

2. Realism: In an effort to derive interpretations for some of the more arcane movements in kata, practitioners will sometimes come up with explanations that would be unlikely to work in practical application, at least in all but the most specific and unusual circumstances. When this happens, it is a strong indicator that the better course lies elsewhere. There are no shortcuts, and it sometimes takes years of study before the correct route to the intended destination reveals itself;

3. Repetition: While a certain amount of repetition in the practice of kata is inevitable—even desirable, as in the case of bilateral practice or cumulative techniques—the correct interpretation is rarely: "more of the same." This is true both within a particular form, and in assessing the value of forms practice as a whole. In other words, each kata (or series of kata) in the art's syllabus should serve a specific and discrete purpose.

♦ **Taikyoku—Stance and Speed:** These forms are meant to teach stance and speed. If the stances and steps are performed perfectly, these forms will end at the exact same spot as they began. In addition, the first form in this series has twenty-one moves, and the last has more than double that number. Yet as the student advances, each version is expected to be performed in the same twenty-one second interval. As a result, the practitioner cannot help but become that much faster over time.

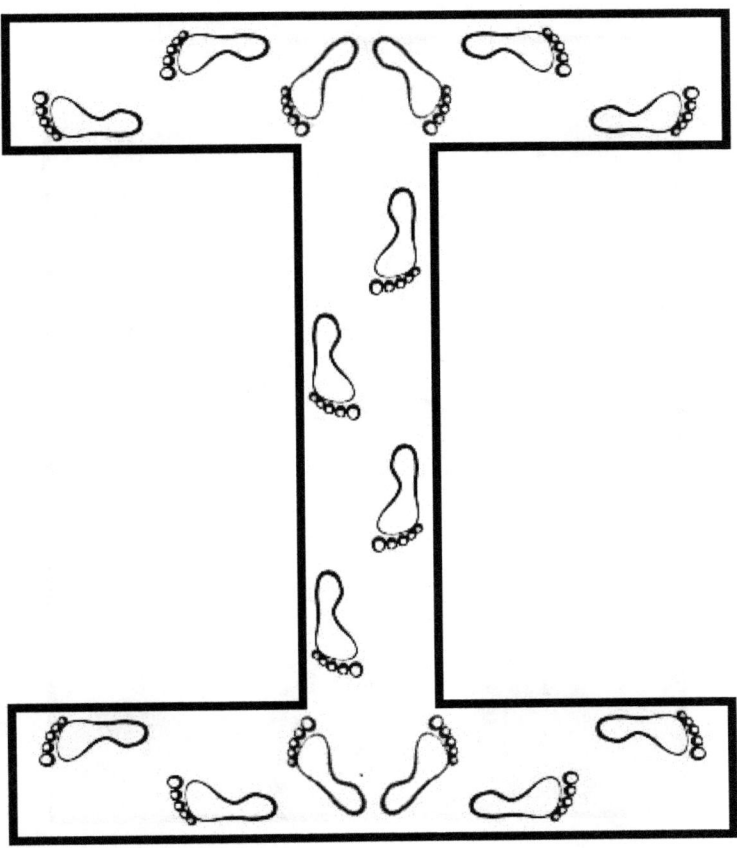

> In these forms you are turning left and right, and spinning in your stances. When I test people on these forms, they must start on a dime, and finish within one foot-width of that dime. That helps to teach you proper stances. If you don't have the proper stance for each of those moves, you won't end up in the same place. By the time you move onto Seisan, you'll have that basic stance down.
>
> —GMGD

♦ **Seisan, Seuichin, Naihanchi, Sanchin—Breathing:** Almost every move in kata Seisan is accompanied by a breath up until the final sequence. Seuichin, by contrast allows the practitioner only three breaths, and the shortest interval in this form is equal to the longest in the previous one. At more advanced levels, kata Naihanchi is performed in one breath (or rather, no breaths, since the practitioner exhales fully before beginning). And kata Sanshin is in many ways the ultimate breathing form. It teaches the student to control the breath and use it to generate internal power.

> ### NAIHANCHI: A SPECIAL RELATIONSHIP
>
> In addition to its role in the sequence of forms that instruct and condition the practitioner's breathing, Naihanchi serves another critical function in the Ryūkyū Kempo syllabus. It is a shibboleth of sorts for students of this style, and a common proving ground for testing their knowledge and understanding of the art. According to Grandmaster Dillman: "Shigeru Nakamura knew one-hundred and ten different moves from just this kata. It's one of the most powerful self-defense kata there are!"

- **Bassai—Fighting Left-handed:** It is said that the originator of this form was left-handed. That is why so many of its moves, like the initial hammer fist for example, favor a southpaw.

- **Chinto—Balance:** It is fairly obvious from its unique characteristics that this form focuses on balance, speed and quick shifting of positions.

- **Kusanku—Combat Form:** This form prioritizes combat applications—not just for the ring, but also for the battlefield. It is said that the moves contained in this kata were so powerful and complicated that it was ultimately broken down into the five Pinans, each of which focuses on a different aspect of the original form.

- **Gojushiho—Energetics:** As might be expected, advanced kata like Gojushiho begin to touch on more esoteric concepts, like the importance of recognizing and reacting to the opponent's energy.

- **Ananku—Weapons Form:** This form ties the empty-handed and weapons-based aspects of Ryūkyū Kempo together beautifully because it lends itself so nicely to performance using virtually all of the traditional kobudo weapons.

- **Niseishi—Killing Form:** It is said that this relatively short form contains almost no defensive techniques, and that each move, even standing alone, is potentially deadly.

- **Kinken—Master Form:** Traditionally taught only at Fifth Dan and above, this form delves deeply into the most advanced aspects of the art, including the role of stances, polarity, and internal energy in combat situations.

Ryūkyū Kempo

◆ THE BUNKAI ALPHABET ◆

Bunkai—the art of decoding centuries-old kata to reveal the treasures they contain—requires dedication, imagination, and sometimes even inspiration. There are, however, several guiding lights in this process; principles that help illuminate the deep truths contained within seemingly mundane movements.

◆ **A—Anthology:** Kata is an anthology of techniques and principles, not just a "dance". As Chris Thomas says, it *shows* you what to do or *tells* you how to do it.

◆ **B—Blocks:** There are none. What are commonly called "blocks" are actually different techniques altogether.[1]

◆ **C—C-step:** Steps often represent kicks, sweeps, reaps, and other kinds of leg techniques.

◆ **D—Deep Stances/Low Moves:** Deep stances and low moves often represents throws, groundwork, or a downed opponent.

◆ **E—Eyes:** The eyes generally look toward the origin of the attack.

◆ **F—Fist:** A clenched fist often represents the *opponent's* punch or grab.

◆ **G—Grouping:** Sequences of techniques are often grouped together by breathing.

◆ **H—Hidden Meaning:** Moves are hidden in kata, but not disguised. Motion and application should match.

◆ **I—Is the move the technique or the transition?**

◆ **J—Jumps:** Jumps often represent throws.

◆ **K—Kiai:** Kiai often signals a finishing technique.

◆ **L—Locks:** Look for the locks in kata.

◆ **M—Multiple Interpretations:** "One inch of movement, five interpretations."

---

[1]. Both Hohan Soken and Seiyu Oyata taught that there are no "blocks" in forms practice. These moves help to build timing and distance skills. —GMGD

- **N—Name:** The name of the form often provides its meaning—or close to its meaning (or even the name of the originator or his family).

- **O—Open Hand:** Open hand techniques often represent a block followed by a grab.

- **P—Pressure Points:** Kata moves often show the location, angle, and direction for pressure point strikes.

- **Q—Quick and Slow:** Slow moves often signal very complex or internally focused techniques.

- **R—Retractions:** There are no mere "retractions"; like "blocks," these are techniques in and of themselves.

- **S—Strikes:** "Strikes" are often blocks (deflections), just as "blocks" are usually strikes.

- **T—Turns:** Turns often represent throws.

- **U—Unilateral techniques:** Moves performed *only* on the left or right generally work better on that side.

- **V—Variations:** Each move has a basic level, a hidden version, and a number of variations.[*Oyo*—the application; *kakushi*—the hidden meaning; *henka*—the variations.]

- **W—Wide Versus Close Grip:** Wide hands often represent spreading the opponent's limbs (as to displace the guard) while close hands usually represent compressing them (as with a lock).

- **X—eXtraneous Moves:** There are none. Even the salutation has meaning.

- **Y—Your Limbs:** Your limbs often represent the *opponent's* limbs.

- **Z—Zanshin:** "Without intent, technique is hollow."

—Hidetaka Nishayama

> If you look deeply enough, you will find wisdom, even if it was not there to begin with.
>
> —The Master

Ryūkyū Kempo

CHAPTER FIVE:
Kumite

Boxing juggernaut Mike Tyson once said, "Everyone has a plan until they get punched in the face." Nineteenth century military strategist Carl Von Clausewitz wrote somewhat more eloquently about "the fog of war." But both warriors were expressing a similar concept: Even the most carefully drafted plans often fall victim to events on the ground. As a result, *resilience* is one of the most important assets in the practitioner's portfolio.

1. Taking a Punch: The expression "glass-jawed" has been around for almost as long as the art of western boxing, and is used to describe a fighter who can't stand up to a solid punch. The opposite—a fighter like George Chuvalo, for example, who is seemingly impervious to a hailstorm of powerful blows—might be called, "iron-jawed."

Whatever someone's natural predisposition in this regard may be, however, experience is a powerful conditioner. In other words, the first time someone gets struck in earnest, it tends to induce a state of shock, if only because it is such a new and overwhelming experience. On the other hand, when a person has become accustomed to taking hits and pressing on in the face of such distractions, the impact of this kind of assault is greatly reduced. Accordingly, the experience of being hit and learning to keep battling on is one of the most powerful lessons that arts have to offer.

2. Throwing a Punch: The corollary to being able to *take* a punch is being able to *throw* one. As a threshold matter, punching another person without having sufficient training can result in as much—and sometimes more—injury to the striker as the target. It is for this very reason that fractured metacarpals are sometimes referred to as "bar room fractures."

Ryūkyū Kempo

It is equally important to recognize that the act of hitting another human being is a highly unusual occurrence in modern, adult society. While people might witness cinematic versions of such behavior being played out on screen all the time, when confronted with the reality of having to engage in such activity, experience is the best teacher.

3. Timing a Punch: Physiatrists tell us that reaction time in humans is largely a product of the ratio of fast-twitch to slow-twitch muscles. There is little that can be done to alter these natural ingredients. Well-trained fighters, however, have learned that there are ways to maximize their existing speed by careful controlling timing, position, and direction.

At an elementary level, throwing a feint to one target—say the right temple—and then following it with a strike to the opposite quadrant—here let's say the left floating rib—can serve to draw the defenses so far from the intended destination on that they simply can't double back in time. At a more advanced level, the creation of, and subsequent deviation from, a natural rhythm can serve first to lull the opponent into a misplaced sense of confidence, and then rudely awaken him from it.

> A feint must also be a strike; a strike, a feint.
> —The Master

4. Avoiding a Punch: It is a fundamental tenet of Ryūkyū Kempo that what are commonly thought of as "blocks" in kata are something else altogether. "Blocking" with force-against-force is inefficient. It is better to deflect than to block; to parry than to deflect; and to avoid than to parry.

> The best "block" is don't be there…
> —The Master

5. Packing a Punch: Newtonian physics tell us that force is a product of mass and acceleration. Both of these variables, however, can be amplified greatly by using the entire body to deliver a strike. The feet grip the surface on which the fighter stands; the legs drive power up to the torso; the hips pivot with the execution of the technique; the arm lashes forward like a whip; and the fist clenches into an iron weight upon impact.

These are just a few guiding principles that may be helpful in the context of free-fighting. There are many others, but, like most things of value in this realm, their lessons are better learned by *doing* than by *reading*. There is no substitute for time served on the mat…

Ryūkyū Kempo

CHAPTER SIX:
Kobudo

The term "karate" means "empty hand." However, many—but not all—systems of Okinawan martial arts also include weapons components. In addition to the direct, tactical value of learning methods of armed combat using a variety of tools, there is also a more indirect benefit to this practice, in that the use of weapons can inform and help perfect certain aspects of empty-handed technique.

Nowhere do these twinned interests find such powerful expression as in the Filipino art of Modern Arnis. The cane is at the same time both a highly-effective self-defense weapon and an invaluable teaching tool. And while the Arnis cane is not, strictly speaking, a traditional Okinawan weapon,[2] Ryūkyū Kempo practitioners the world over have benefited greatly from the warm association and exchange of techniques and ideas over the years between the headmasters of these two systems.

The traditional Okinawan weapons—as opposed to those imported from other styles—are said to have evolved from farming tools adapted for combat by the region's disarmed inhabitants during the Japanese occupation of the island nation that spanned nearly three centuries (1609-1879). While there are something like a dozen different tools in this particular box, the following section examines only those that comprise a significant part of the Ryūkyū Kempo syllabus.

♦ **Bo (Staff):** This six-foot long wooden staff was likely derived from a tool called a *"tenbin"*—a pole laid across the shoulders to carry pails or baskets hooked on either end. It is considered the "king" of weapons, and is the first one learned by many karate-ka. It would be difficult to find a senior Ryūkyū Kempo practitioner who didn't have at least passing familiarity with the principles and techniques of this tool. Several bo kata even feature in the syllabus of this art, and many of the principles governing the use of this weapon are equally applicable to variants like the shorter *jo* staff or the pointed spear *(yari)*.

♦ **Nunchaku (Flail):** This weapon, consisting of two short sticks joined by a metal chain or leather thong, is thought to have evolved from a rice flail. It was a favorite of the late Bruce Lee, and, as a result of his association with George Dillman (together with extensive training from Jim Coffman), features prominently in the Ryūkyū Kempo syllabus, with various techniques and several forms often being taught to senior practitioners. The principles governing the use of a hinged weapon of this kind are markedly different from those that apply to wielding a staff.

♦ **Kama (Sickle):** These hand-held sickles come in pairs, and do not differ significantly in form and function from the farm tools from which they evolved. These were favorites of Hohan Soken, and, as a result of his association with George Dillman, also feature in the Ryūkyū Kempo syllabus, with various techniques and several forms often being taught to senior practitioners.

[2.] Despite obvious similarities in form and use to the Okinawan *tanbo*.

HOHAN SOKEN'S KAMA DEMONSTRATION

Hohan Soken grew up as a boy throwing kama (as boys might throw knives in this country) from the age of four. He did a demonstration for us with an audience of two thousand at a hotel in Pittsburgh where his student Fusei Kise had to run around with a wooden target while Soken threw kama at him. There was nothing to protect the audience from the kama, and we tried to talk him out of doing the demonstration. We told him that there were people all around and the insurance wouldn't cover it if he missed.

He said, "No miss."

I didn't want to say, "You're eighty-three and we're worried!" We couldn't talk him out of it!

> So out comes Fusei Kise on stage holding his board and the rest of us sat there holding our breath! Hohan Soken picked up about eight or ten sharp, heavy sickles. He began throwing them and we were all counting down for each sickle. Then he started picking up the timing. Finally he got down to the last one. It hit the board. We all let out a sigh of relief and he got a standing ovation. Then he goes over and picks up more kama. His student announces that Sensei will now demonstrate kata with the kama.
>
> Soken began doing the form. Toward the end he turns to the main part of the audience, lets out a kiai and throws one of the kama right at them. There's no Fusei Kise there! Some of the audience dropped to the floor. Some ducked into the aisle. What nobody knew—including us—was that he had a cord on the kama, with the other end locked to his thumb. It went spinning out about ten feet into the air. It didn't fall, but ended in a perfect "stick" position. And with one snap, he pulled it straight back into his hand. The place went nuts!
>
> —GMGD

- **Tonfa (Baton):** These batons have perpendicular handles closer to one end than the other, and are generally used in pairs. They are thought to have evolved from handles used to turn millstones. In form and function they closely resemble the side-handled batons used by police. Given George Dillman's experience as a military policeman in the Service, and his subsequent work with law enforcement agencies of all kinds, it is a fitting choice for inclusion in the Ryūkyū Kempo syllabus. George Dillman credits Sam Pearson and Fusei Kise with teaching him this weapon, and he himself passes on its techniques and forms to some of his senior students.

- **Sai (Trident):** These hand-held metal tridents have a long central prong flanked by two shorter ones, and are also typically used in pairs. They may have evolved from planting or furrowing tools. George Dillman credits Harry Smith and Greg Lindquist with teaching him this weapon, and he himself passes on its techniques and forms to some of his senior students.

WEAPONS MASTERY

It should be noted that in addition to the individual instruction described above, George Dillman was awarded a Fifth *Dan* in Okinawan Kobudo by Masanao Takazawa in 1970, specifically noting his mastery in the fighting methods and forms of all five of the weapons described above.

Ryūkyū Kempo

There are several other traditional Okinawan weapons, including *tekko* (steel-knuckles), *tinbe-rochin* (shield and spear), *surujin* (weighted chain), *tanbo* (short stick), *hanbo* (mid-length staff) and *eku* (oar), but the ones described in greater detail above are the primary tools of the Ryūkyū Kempo practitioner

Like Arnis canes, the *katana* is not a traditional Okinawan weapon, although its origins are somewhat closer to the Ryūkyū islands than the Philippines. Nevertheless, George Dillman learned the use of this weapon from Daniel Pai, and has passed this knowledge on to select students over the years.

> In time, the hands become weapons; the body, armor.
>
> —The Master

CHAPTER SEVEN:
Kyusho-jitsu

Acupuncture—the art of healing by stimulating any of hundreds of points on the human body—has been practiced in China for thousands of years, and was relatively well-known in the west by the 1970s.

What was less well-known, at least until George Dillman began teaching it openly, was *Kyusho-jitsu*—the concomitant ability to inflict pain and other forms of harm using these same points. There are some who do not approve of the Promethean dissemination of this once-secret knowledge, but its impact on the martial arts community is undeniable.

Kyusho-jitsu exists, and can be employed, alongside the study of vital points and nerve striking, but it is a qualitatively different phenomenon.

♦ **Vital Points:** As used in this text, the term "vital points," refers to structurally vulnerable parts of the body, such as the temples, eyes, eardrums, throat, clavicles, floating ribs, groin, knee, instep, and so on. While these are undoubtedly effective targets for the martial artist, and often coincide with the location of pressure points, they are not the same thing.

♦ **Nerve Points:** Similarly, western medicine—like the cadaver studies George Dillman undertook with Dr. Ralph Buschbacher in the 1980s—recognizes that the body's observable nervous system has certain sensitive spots, like the mental nerve, the brachial plexus, and the ulnar nerve (funny bone). Again, while these networks and clusters are often valid striking targets, and frequently overlap with the location of acupuncture points, they are not synonymous.

◆ **Pressure Points:** Acupuncture theory posits that there are more than four hundred separate, discernable points spread out across the body along twelve meridians and eight vessels, and that stimulation of these points—individually or in groups—can have an immediate and powerful effect on a the body.

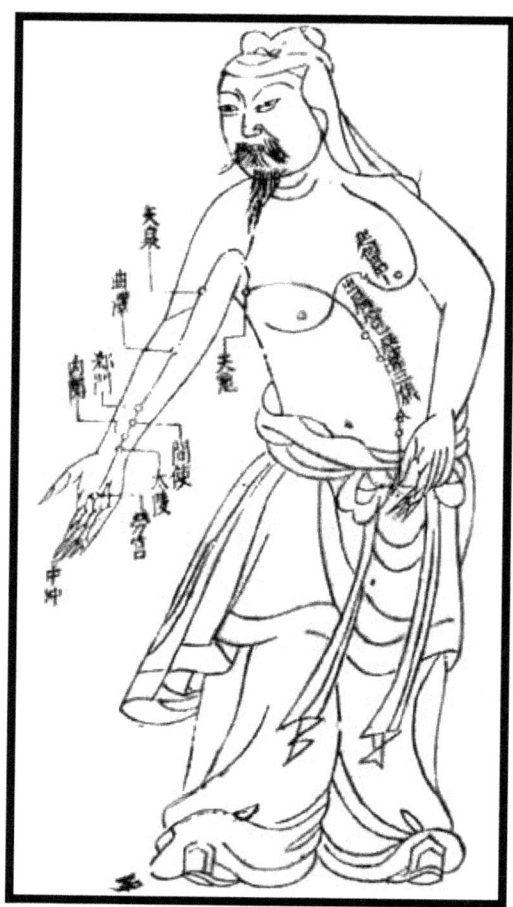

The angle, direction, and method employed in activating particular points can dramatically affect the outcome. When striking multiple points, either parallel or in series, *yin-yang* polarity, elemental cycles, and even the diurnal sequence can help determine the most effective pattern to employ. And it is no accident that many striking sequences seen in kata fit these models exactly.

At a superficial level, every martial artist can benefit from learning a few, key, pressure points and the effects that they can reliably induce.

For example:

- **Liver-9:** When struck, ideally with a stepover kick, this point on the inside of the thigh will reliably buckle the supporting leg.

- **Lung-5:** When struck (or pressed), this point on the inside of the forearm will reliably buckle the opponent's knees. The angle of the attack is a C-shape that bows out toward the opponent but then cuts back toward the practitioner.

- **Large Intestine-10:** When struck (or pressed), this point on the outside of the forearm will numb the arm and turn the head away.

- **Stomach-25:** When pressed (or struck), these points on either side of the navel will reliably bend the opponent's torso.

- **Spleen-6:** When struck (or pressed), this point on the inside of the ankle will reliably weaken the opponent's stance.

- **Heart-6:** When pressed, this point on the ulnar aspect of the inside of the wrist will reliably bend the opponent's wrist. This point is often hooked and twisted toward the hand.

- **Small Intestine-18:** When pressed (or struck) in an upward direction, this point in the hollow of the cheek will reliably release the neck, forcing the head up and back.

- **Bladder-57:** When pressed—especially when the opponent is prone—this point in the middle of the back of the calf will exert extreme pain.

- **Kidney-26:** When struck at a downward angle, this point just below the clavicle will exert tremendous pain/numbness in the chest.

- **Pericardium-6:** When pressed, this point on the inside of the wrist will reliably weaken the opponent's grip. The direction of pressure is toward the hand.

- **Triple Warmer-11:** When rubbed, this point behind the elbow will release the shoulder and allow the arm to be hyperextended, facilitating an arm lock.

- **Gall Bladder-20:** When these points in the vicinity of the occipital protuberance are struck in an upward direction, dizziness and unconsciousness will often result.

> A true master can topple the mountain with his fingertips, because he knows where to push.
> —The Master

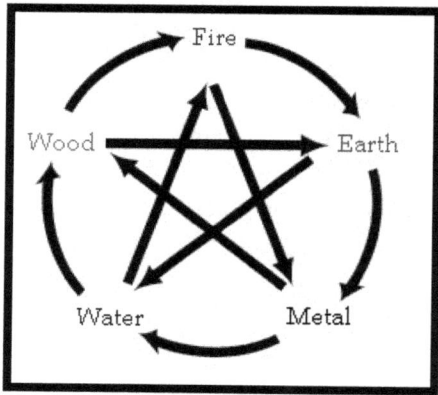

Delving a little deeper, acupuncture theory can reveal not only the location of pressure points, but also patterns of application that will induce specific reactions that might not have been discovered by trial-and-error, including rendering the opponent unconscious with minimal force.

For example:

- **Heart-6/Lung-5/Gall Bladder 13, 14, & 15:** If an opponent pushes or seizes the practitioner in the vicinity of the lapels, grabbing and controlling the attacker's wrist at the crease will reliably trigger Heart-6 (a fire point). Dropping an elbow on the offending forearm next is a convenient follow-up technique that will usually stimulate Lung-5 (a metal point). And completing the pattern by striking the opponent's forehead with a palm will hit the Gall Bladder 13, 14 & 15 cluster (wood points).

This sequence follows the elemental Cycle of Destruction. It is also anatomically sound, mechanically viable, defensively effective, and likely to daze or otherwise disable the attacker safely. In addition, it tracks the opening sequence of a particular Ryūkyū Kempo form very closely.

Granted, not every point or combination will work on every opponent, every time, but studying the underlying theory gives the practitioner access to a target-rich treasure map rather than simply sending him back to a handful of known 'deposits.' And where, as here, the martial artist can have access to both, it makes sense to mine this particular vein of knowledge for all it's worth…

☉	☯	☆	⏱	Method/Effect
LV-9	●	🌲	01-03	Hit/buckles knee
LU-5	●	✕	03-05	Hit/buckles knee
LI-10	○	✕	05-07	Hit/numb arm, turn head
ST-25	○	⊕	07-09	Press/weakens posture
SP-6	●	⊕	09-11	Hit/weakens stance
HT-6	●	🔥	11-13	Press/weakens wrist
SI-18	○	🔥	13-15	Press/releases neck
BL-37	○	🔥	15-17	Press/incapacitate leg
KI-26	●	🔥	17-19	Hit/incapacitates chest
PC-6	●	🔥	19-21	Press/weakens fist
TW-11	○	🔥	21-23	Rub/hyperextend elbow
GB-20	○	🌲	23-01	Hit/knock out point

Ryūkyū Kempo

CHAPTER EIGHT:
The Rubicon

This is the point in the journey where the path divides and the reader must choose which way to proceed.

Embarking on the study of any true martial art is the voyage of a lifetime. If the student simply wishes to learn how to defend himself, this goal can be achieved in weeks or months. It does not require years or decades.

If the student is just looking for a way to keep fit, then what he is pursuing is a hobby—no different than, say, golf or racquetball.

But for those who are truly seeking membership in an ancient warrior tradition, their course of study will run both long and deep.

Over the centuries and millennia, great warriors have dedicated their lives to researching the martial arts, so it is not surprising that there are layers upon layers of knowledge and understanding to be discovered. This process takes time. But it also requires that the student keeps an open mind.

There was a time when the ideas of a round earth or a heliocentric solar system were dismissed as nonsense by the greater part of the scientific community. But this did not make them wrong.

In addition, the process of pushing back the boundaries of the known world will often give rise to the odd misstep along the way. This does not make it futile.

On the contrary, a true master should do more than simply perform the existing techniques of his system exquisitely. He should seek to add something to them. To advance the inquiry. To leave things a little better than he found them.

There are some styles in which the headmaster's function is simply to teach the classes. There are others where this responsibility is entrusted to the senior disciples over time, thereby allowing the most experienced practitioners to explore new possibilities; to experiment with that which has yet to be perfected or even proven; to innovate, or even to re-discover forgotten ideas and principles. And so each student must decide whether to stick to the well-worn path, or venture out into the undiscovered country.

Eastern cosmology is based on a number of principles that are simply not present in its western counterpart: The interconnectedness of the Dao. The bifurcation of this unitary concept into the symbiotic relationship of yin and yang. The further subdivision and characterization of all things according to the law of the five elements. The mysterious power of chi. These are all concepts that permeate almost every aspect of Chinese and Japanese culture, including medicine and the other so-called hard sciences.

In fact, no true understanding of many, or indeed most, Eastern disciplines can be had without at least some understanding and appreciation of these concepts. Yet until recently, these ideas were conspicuously absent from martial arts teachings in the United States and elsewhere. Thanks to pioneers like George Dillman, this is no longer the case.

> There are more things in heaven and earth… Than are dreamt of in your philosophy.
>
> —The Bard

CHAPTER NINE:
Through the Looking Glass

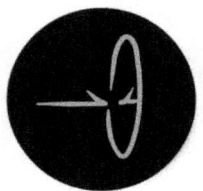

Many martial historians believe that U.S. servicemen stationed in Japan following the Second World War were taught to employ the full-twist punch more as a safety measure than an effective combat technique. This is so, at least in part, because the surface area of the fist when striking the opponent's chest in this manner tends to overlap with multiple ribs, whereas the diamond shape of a three-quarter punch penetrates into such vital regions as the solar plexus, potentially damaging fragile structures like the Xiphoid Process, and its angle allows it to target individual ribs.

If this is so, then it begs the question, "how many other aspects of that early martial dogma were made deliberately misleading for any number of reasons?" According to Dillman, the short answer is, "most of them."

> In the beginning I realized that everybody had been taught these different moves following World War Two, basically being taught by the people they had just defeated. So I tried doing these same moves in different ways, and found that there were ways to work them better. In fact, sometimes it took doing the exact opposite of what the servicemen had been taught. If they were had been taught to hit up, I would hit down. If they had been taught to strike left, I'd strike right. If they had been taught to twist inside, I would twist to the outside. And it worked. But this was only the beginning.

Ryūkyū Kempo

> Even the three-quarter punch—the more dangerous way is to reverse it, twisting to the *outside*. You can knock someone out with that by striking to the hole in the middle of the cheek—small intestine, but heart is there deep down...
>
> —GMGD

As a result, Ryūkyū Kempo practitioners are taught specific methods for best employing a variety of hand-weapons. For example:

- Index Knuckle Fist—Strike Down
- Hammer Fist—Strike Down
- Shuto—Strike Down
- Empi—Strike Down or Up
- Back Fist—Strike Down or Up
- Reverse Hammer Fist—Strike Up
- Middle Knuckle Fist—Strike Up
- Three-quarter punch—Strike In (Penetrating)

CHAPTER TEN:
Angle, Direction, & Method

Anyone who has had the misfortune to hit the "funny bone" on a hard surface knows the debilitating and disproportionate amount of pain and numbness that this simple action can cause. They also know that the activation of this point depends in large part on the angle at which it is struck, and often on the precise amount of force with which contact is made—neither too much nor too little. Where too little force can be insufficient to make the blow register at all, paradoxically, too much can drown out the particular sensation that a glancing blow of moderate force can cause.

Practitioners of pressure point theory—whether they be martial artists or acupuncturist—recognize that the angle and direction, as well as the method of application, of a strike can change the effect of that strike dramatically.

> Hohan Soken and Seiyu Oyata both taught me that it mattered what angle and direction you would strike a pressure point. Up until this point, people thought it just mattered that you knew where the point was. As we learned more and more, we found out that the direction of the strike mattered as well as the type of strike. Was it a hit point? A rub point? A touch point? These things made a big difference.
>
> —GMGD

Ryūkyū Kempo

Some common examples of this principle at play in Ryūkyū Kempo teachings, using just the Triple Warmer ("TW") meridian for illustrative purposes, include:

- TW-3—Press Point, Perpendicular (90°);
- TW-6, 7, 8—Touch (Grind) or Hit Point, Perpendicular (90°);
- TW-11—Rub Point (up-down), Perpendicular (90°);
- TW-12— Hit Point, Perpendicular (90°);
- TW-17—Strike, Oblique (45°, back to front);
- TW-23—Strike, Oblique (60°, back to front).

CHAPTER ELEVEN:
Polarity & Quadrants

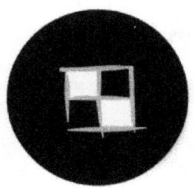

Any true understanding of the traditional Eastern martial arts depends on developing an appreciation for the fundamental universal cosmology on which those cultures are based. In the various Eastern countries, it is a widely-held belief that yin and yang[3] arise together from an initial emptiness (*wuji*), and continue moving in tandem until a state of equilibrium is reached again.

A useful analogy for illustrating this idea is the thought of dropping a stone into still waters. Waves and troughs will radiate from the point of the initial disturbance, moving in sequence with one another, until eventually the surface of the water will grow still once more.

[3.] Yin and yang are the Chinese terms; in and yo are the Japanese counterparts.

Ryūkyū Kempo

While the concepts of yin and yang are almost impossible to define, yin is often characterized as slow, soft, yielding, diffuse, cold, wet, or tranquil, and is associated with water, earth, the moon, femininity and nighttime.

Yang, by contrast, is fast, hard, solid, focused, hot, dry, or aggressive, and is associated with fire, sky, the sun, masculinity and daytime.

Whether or not a Western student of the Eastern arts actually subscribes to this world view, he must at least *appreciate* it if he is ever to achieve a deep understanding of his subject matter.

And whether it is polarity, or some other phenomenon, that accounts for the disproportionately powerful effect on a male combatant of being struck on his right side (yang) by another man (same polarity) using a right back fist (yin), the result speaks for itself.

> I first studied polarity with Danny Pai. He talked about it over dinner with me and Bruce Lee. He explained the idea that there is a kind of "electricity" in the body, there are positive and negative sides, and striking on one side and then the other works better.
>
> Seiyu Oyata explained more about this same theory. He was the one who talked about dividing the body down the middle as though it was cut with a sword. Right side is positive (for males). The left side is negative. Right (male) open hand is positive. Left (male) open hand is negative. So the strongest weapons you can strike with are right palm and left fist. You can prove this by grabbing or striking at the proper place with the proper hand weapon. And if you lift your heel in a cat stance, you can reverse the polarity. This also plays into quadrant theory.
>
> —GMGD

Accordingly, Ryūkyū Kempo teaches that the human body's polarity is as follows:

- Front—Positive
- Back—Negative
- Top—Positive
- Bottom—Negative
- Right—Positive (Male)
- Left—Negative (Male)

Ryūkyū Kempo

CHAPTER TWELVE:
The Power of Breath

Any strenuous physical activity causes the respiratory process to quicken. Paradoxically, fear can inhibit this process, as anyone who has experienced shortness of breath before delivering a speech to a crowded room can attest. How, then, is the martial artist to safeguard this vital process in the face of both the exertion and apprehension that typically accompanies a fight? The answer is by learning to control his breathing; a process which is both assisted by, and necessary to, the practice of meditation.

For this reason alone, the study of breath control is a vital weapon in any martial artist's armamentarium. But there are deeper reasons as well. Among these is the fact that the respiratory process links the conscious mind and the autonomic system in a unique and powerful way. By learning to control his breathing, the martial artist can begin to tap into the awesome power of the unconscious mind.

> I learned breathing from Danny Pai and also from Isshin Ryu. As Harry Smith explained, the order of the first few kata in Isshin Ryu are intended to teach you breathing. But later, from my research, I came to realize things like when you breathe in, you weaken your chi, and when you breathe out, you strengthen it. But you also weaken and strengthen your opponent's energy in the same way, so you need to be careful with this. Breathing is closely related to kiai, and is even part of it.
> —GMGD

Ryūkyū Kempo

CHAPTER THIRTEEN:
Kiai—The Power of Sound

The power of sound has been an enduring tenet of Eastern cosmology since its inception. For example, according to the Kotodoma, "Su" was the first sound in—and indeed of—creation.

Those who interpret the well-known concept of *kiai* as being nothing more than a "spirit yell," have missed the point entirely. The ancient samurai texts teach that a master of *kiaijutsu* can fell a bird in flight with the power of sound; it is scientific fact that a trained opera singer can shatter a glass using her voice; and it is modern reality that sound technology is already being used as a weapon in military, police, and intelligence fields in many different countries.

> Even in the beginning we were taught to yell, but we weren't taught *what* to yell, *how* to yell or *why* to yell. Seiyu Oyata taught this. For example, he demonstrated using a "eh" sound in Naihanchi. There is even a videotape of one of Seiyu Oyata's teachers yelling and making people drop the weapons they're holding! When I first saw this, I wasn't sure I even believed it. But as I got more and more into it, Oyata explained that it's like listening to a radio during a thunderstorm. When there's a flash of lightening, the sound goes out for a second. The kiai interrupts the flow of energy in the body like a storm.

> When you kiai a certain way, it affects the energy of that organ. There's a sound for every element, every organ, every angle, and every direction. But you do not use the cycle of destruction with sound. If you use a "metal" sound, strike a metal point. You don't use a "fire" sound to strike a metal point (even though fire melts metal). Element-to-element works better (whereas with some of the other enhancers, cycle of destruction works better).
>
> There are sounds for close range and medium range (inside or outside what some people call "the aura"). Some sounds are healing sounds and some sounds are meant to hurt...
>
> —GMGD

Consider the attention-getter/warning, "Hey!" in the United States and "Oi!" in England. Similar 'barks' are used by members of the human and animal kingdoms the world over and across cultures to shock and deter. And one of the early stages in the "force continuum" embraced by law enforcement agencies is "voice command." To dismiss the value of such sonic weaponry is to have an incomplete arsenal...

Ryūkyū Kempo

<u>The Basics</u>:

- Sideways—"Eh" [usually a rising tone—"e-eh!"]
- Down—"Kyu" [may sound like the "-choo" part of a sneeze]
- Forward—"Ho" [like a short "oh" with a breathy beginning]
- Up—"Ah" [usually a split/rising tone—"aa-ah!"]
- Internal—"Hee" [like a hiss]
- Retreating/defending—"Sa" [usually a hissing, split tone—"sa-ah!"]
- Back—"Ng" [like a glottal stop]

NAIHANCHI

It is interesting to note that if the practitioner performs all three Naihanchi forms in sequence, they contain side strikes ("E-eh!"); Downward strikes ("Kyu!"); Forward strikes ("Ho!"); and upward strikes ("Aa-ah!"). In addition, if the practitioner inserts a sidestep left between forms two and three—as is commonly done to ensure that the end point is the same as the start point—then that may be considered an internal ("Hee") and/or retreating/defending ("Sa") move…

<u>Advanced Practice</u>:

- Fire—"Kee"
- Metal—"See"
- Wood—"Shu"
- Earth—"Her"
- Water—"Pa"

CHAPTER FOURTEEN:
Stance

It is indisputable that body-mechanics have a significant impact on all manner of athletic endeavors. Professional athletes enlist the aid of scientists from a variety of disciplines in searching for ways to shave a few seconds off their time, or add a couple of inches to their jump. It should therefore come as no surprise that the way in which a martial artists holds his body can have a tremendous effect on the power of his techniques. Whether this phenomenon is attributable to western laws of physics or Eastern cosmological theories is largely irrelevant to the result. The fact is, *it works*.[4]

> It's the same with your stance. Oyata taught that too. Most people don't understand why they practice stances. They tell you, "horse stance is for fighting sideways." The truth is that each stance is associated with an element. For instance, a fire stance will hurt a fire point even more, and a metal point more than that. You need to know what each stance means in terms of the elements.
>
> —GMGD

[4.] See Amy Cuddy's Ted Talk on the effect of power poses.

Ryūkyū Kempo

- Fire—Front Stance
- Metal—Cat Stance
- Wood—Seiuchin Stance
- Earth—Horse Stance
- Water—Cross Stance[5]

> **The Law of the Five Elements**—*Gogyo* in Japanese; *Wu Xing* in Chinese—is a system for describing the relationships between, and interactions among, a wide variety of phenomena. It has been employed for centuries as an analytical, and even predictive, tool in such disparate fields as Traditional Chinese Medicine, Martial Arts, Military Strategy, Feng Shui, Astrology and even Music. The elements in question are: Fire, Water, Earth, Metal and Wood, and they can be arranged in either a destructive or a constructive sequence, depending on the intention of the practitioner.

[5.] Can be by crossing with own or *opponent's* leg.

CHAPTER FIFTEEN:
Colors

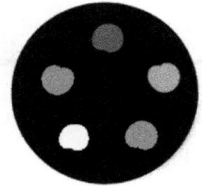

It has been conclusively established in the Western scientific community that exposure to certain colors can have a profound effect on a person's psychological condition. Perhaps the best known example of this is the use of Baker-Miller pink (named for two US Naval Officers who discovered this phenomenon) in correctional facilities to calm violent tendencies in prisoners.

According to Dr. Alexander Schauss, the director of the American Institute for Biosocial Research in Tacoma Washington: "Even if a person tries to be angry or aggressive in the presence of pink, he can't. The heart muscles can't race fast enough. It's a tranquilizing color that saps your energy. Even the color-blind are tranquilized by pink rooms."

It should be noted, however, that despite these powerful effect of this phenomenon, the reaction is short term, and once the stimulus is removed, the subject may regress to an even more agitated state.

> Each element is associated with a color. And color can affect the power of the strike too. You can visualize colors when you are doing your techniques. Even the color of the gi can do things to the body (but I don't really look at that in self-defense situations too much). It's kind of like how polyester fabric can weaken the body but 100% cotton can strengthen it. At least a little. —GMGD

Ryūkyū Kempo

- Fire—Red
- Metal—White, Silver, or Gray
- Wood—Green
- Earth—Yellow
- Water—Blue

CHAPTER SIXTEEN:
Extremities

One of the interesting things about the acupuncture meridians—the pathways along which particular points are located—is that they begin or end at a finger or toe.

Beyond this, each finger is associated with a particular element, and the use of these digits—alone or in combination with one another—is said to influence the effect of the action the hand is making. This helps to explain, at least in part, some of the more esoteric techniques taught at very advanced levels to senior practitioners, in a variety of disciplines, from martial arts to palmistry to massage to Reiki.

> Each finger has an element too, and whatever you do with one hand translates to the other. So when you see the kung fu stylist holding his hand one way and striking with the other, he is getting the elements with the fingers of the other hand. Keeping this in mind, your best ridge hand is with your thumb aimed at your middle finger—that's earth to fire with water in the background...
>
> —GMGD

Ryūkyū Kempo

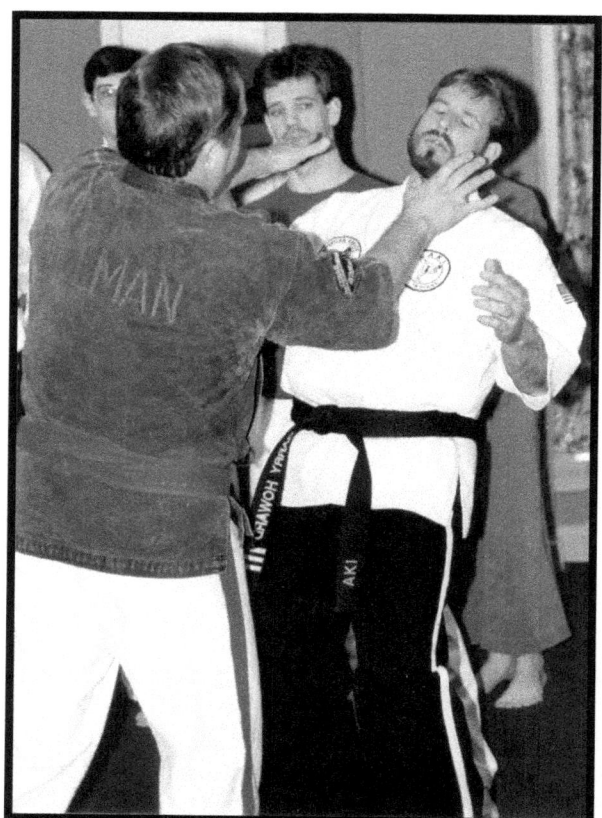

- Fire—Middle
- Metal—Ring
- Wood—Index
- Earth—Thumb
- Water—Pinkie

CHAPTER SEVENTEEN:
Tongue Placement

Physicians and scientists with experience in the realm of traumatic brain injury have documented both the diagnostic and therapeutic effect that tongue placement can have on cognitive functioning, even if only as a byproduct of kinesthetic awareness. Thus, the link between tongue placement and brain function is well established.

The next step in the process—the effect on the body—is a much smaller divide to straddle. As with emotion, brain function can have as great an effect on our ability to perform, and some would argue even greater, than mere physical conditioning. The relaxed, optimistic, and determined state of mind required to perform a difficult break is a familiar concept to the martial artist. And even non-martial artists can appreciate the importance of mind-set in approaching a challenging task.

As with many aspects of this treatment, readers are not expected to accept these theories as conclusively-established facts. Rather, they are encouraged to explore, experience, and experiment with them in order to determine whether they have value, either as a direct result of their validity, or simply because they happen to explain a result that is attributable to some other cause. In other words, just because the ancient Greeks believed that the god Helios towed the sun across the sky each day, did it make the sunrise any less reliable? And it should also be considered that learning to control tongue placement is of value to the martial artist if for no other reason than to avoid biting it off!

> According to the masters, even the position of the tongue in the mouth can be important. For example, pressing the tongue into the water point (directly up and into the soft palate) and stimulating it can cause the production of saliva when the mouth is dry. All of the elements are in the mouth.
>
> —GMGD

- Fire—Gums above the teeth, front of palate;
- Metal—Touch teeth or behind teeth;
- Wood—The palate, behind the fire point;
- Earth— Bottom of mouth behind the lower teeth;
- Water—Straight up onto soft palate.

CHAPTER EIGHTEEN:
Emotion

As with many of the theories presented herein, the proof of the proposition that emotion can effect physical performance can be best appreciated by resort to common experience. A bad mood can affect not only mental functioning, but such things as energy levels, physical dexterity, and even balance. How much more common is it to knock over or break things inadvertently when in a foul mood? In a reciprocal sense, when experiencing the transcendent state of euphoria typically described in sporting terms as, "finding the groove," or "hitting your stride," it seems that the athlete can do no wrong.

> How you're feeling can affect the strength of your technique and I don't just mean if you are confident or scared. A lot of the research on this came from T.A. Frazer. Even Bruce Lee and Wally Jay used to teach that you couldn't be angry in doing technique, and that you couldn't take on the anger of your opponent. You must be like the stone that is thrown into the water—not affected by the ripples. There are three basic emotions: Happy, sad, and angry.
>
> —GMGD

Ryūkyū Kempo

- Fire—Joy
- Metal—Grief
- Wood—Anger
- Earth— All
- [Water—Fear]

- Happiness defeats anger
- Sorrow defeats happiness
- Anger defeats sorrow

CHAPTER NINETEEN:
The Right Tool

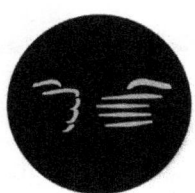

The term, "pressure" is often used inaccurately by martial artists, as in: "it only takes eight pounds of pressure to break the clavicle." An accurate measure of pressure requires the provision of information about *both* the force involved *and* the area to which it is being applied. A more accurate statement might therefore be: "it only takes eight pounds of pressure *per square inch* to break the clavicle."

As a result, the surface area of the striking weapon becomes critical to the inquiry. The net effect of a blow delivered by an open palm, for example, is likely to be much less than a strike of the same strength in which the knuckles are used (assuming all other conditions remain the same). Thus, the martial artist's choice of weapon is critical. Fortunately, there are so many to choose from.

There are many additional theories about the nature and effect of hand (and foot) weapons, including: the Chinese animal system, in which each hand weapon is associated with a particular creature from the wild kingdom; the yin-yang approach; and the omnipresent five element theory.

Ryūkyū Kempo practitioners are armed with a wide choice of tools in this regard, including:

Ryūkyū Kempo

- The standard fist —Thumb over index finger
- Okinawan fist—Index finger extended

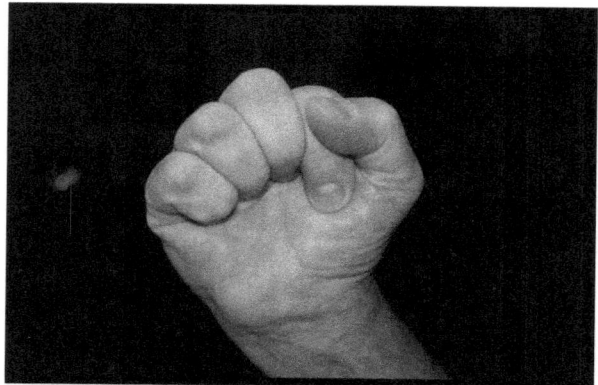

- Index-knuckle fist—For 'rapping' downward
- Middle-knuckle fist—For 'driving' up
- Ridge hand—Thumb aimed at middle finger

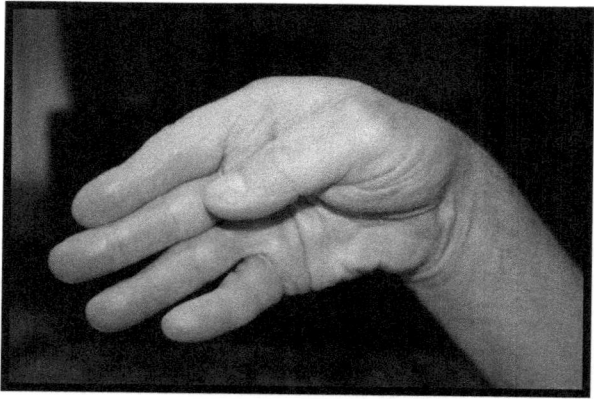

- Shuto—Thumb alongside index finger
- Crane beak—Thumb in center connecting tips of other fingers

CHAPTER TWENTY:
Auras

A master of the martial arts should be more than just an experienced black belt. In other words, as the practitioner matures, there should be a *qualitative*, as well as a *quantitative*, change in his knowledge and understanding.

All too often students of the martial arts work very hard to earn their first black belt, but then do nothing to justify the following promotions beyond more of the same—more basics, more forms, more sparring. And while it is possible to glean wisdom in this fashion, it is a circuitous path to this destination.

While it is vital for the martial artist to remember to pay due respect to his origins, at the higher levels, advanced practitioners should not limit themselves to the basic concepts that informed their initial foray into the martial realm. Rather it is appropriate for them to strive for the horizon and push back the boundaries of what is currently known and understood.

During the 1940s, Semyon Davidovich Kirlian, a Russian inventor and researcher, developed a system of photography that worked using electric current and photographic film, but no actual camera. The images produced by this method showed what appeared to be miniature fireworks displays of light and color playing around the subjects that appeared in them. Kirlian claimed that these were auras, and that Kirlian photography could provide an index of a person's physical health, and illuminate the acupuncture points of the human body.

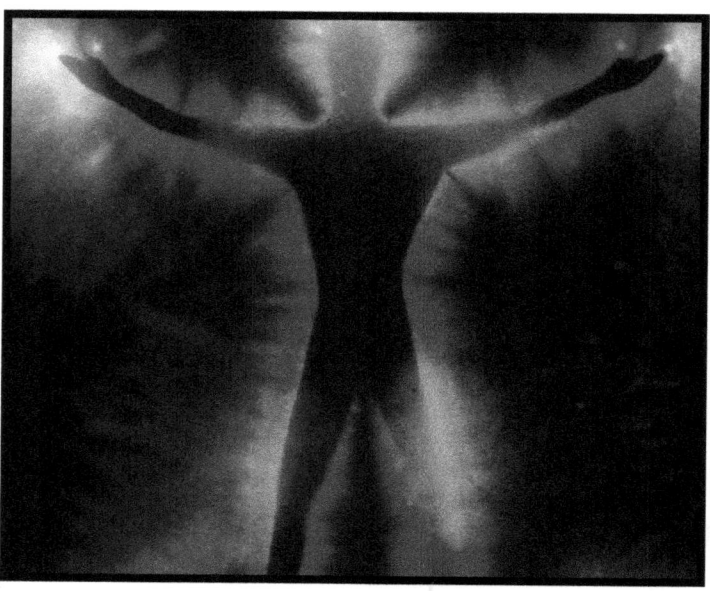

> I learned from Danny Pai that it mattered what your actions were during the argument before the fight—how you could mess up the other guy's aura before even throwing a punch, by reaching into his personal space. There are ways to "rip a hole" in someone else's aura. When you do that, you create a weakness in that place. That's where he's going to fall. There's also a way you can "spin a circle" to protect yourself, hardening your own aura using sound. Some people called it "the iron shirt." I haven't taught this to anybody yet, but you start like this at the *dan t'ien* and picture a spinning whirlpool. Then, when someone tries to attack, you make the appropriate sound…
>
> —GMGD

- "Sa"/"Ha"—Strengthening your own aura
- "Oh"/"Kyu"—Penetrating opponent's aura
- "Ah"/"Eh"—For use outside the aura (up/side)

CHAPTER TWENTY-ONE:
Lo Shu Square

At some point in the journey, a true follower of the way, a seeker of the source, must ask himself if he is content to limit his inquiries to what he can actually see, hear, and touch, or whether he wishes to reach out into the abyss that lies beyond the frontier of the known, for as Hamlet said to Horatio: "There are more things in Heaven and Earth... Than are dreamt of in your philosophy."

This is a part of the martial journey that can only be undertaken on an individual basis and depends as much on faith as it does on empirical observation. Proof is hard to come by in this realm, and this discipline is far more art than science. But in the end, we all must decide for ourselves what kind of world we choose to inhabit...

> Lo Shu Square—this is used in Chinese healing in children's ceremonies, kind of like the Bar Mitzvah ceremony in the Jewish faith. These numbers are drawn on the top of the child's head to open up his channels. It's almost 3,000 years old. It can be done on the hands and the feet as well, to activate the internal energies. You press on the palm or the sole of the foot in the place for the numbers one through four and six through nine—only using five in very serious cases—and it gets the energy

Ryūkyū Kempo

> flowing. It can be done on the top of the head to release a fever. It can be done on the lower belly for stomach pain. If you press on the points with a natural object, it works even better. And to stop it you need to clap or slap them hard. The directions are the same on both hands, even though they are on opposite sides.
>
> —GMGD

4	9	2
3	5	7
8	1	6

CHAPTER TWENTY-TWO:
The Source

Ryūkyū Kempo's connection to the Japanese archipelago from which it sprang is clear. But the development of the Okinawan art—like so many others— was itself informed centuries, if not millennia, ago by ancient Chinese beliefs and martial practices. It was therefore fitting that in 2006, George Dillman and fifty-five of his students traveled to China for two weeks to see and study in the place which, perhaps more than any other, is universally recognized as the source of the eastern martial arts.

Ryūkyū Kempo

Of particular interest and significance was the time they spent at the Shaolin Temple. For centuries the Temple was a gathering place for students and teachers of a variety of martial arts throughout the Far East. Masters of various disciplined trained in those hallowed halls and exchanged principles and techniques, and this spirit of martial sharing endured and migrated to such places as the Camp at Deer Lake.

At the Temple, the visitors met and trained with Senior Monk Shi De Jing. After only a few sessions it became apparent that there were many similarities between the ancient practices of the monks at Shaolin and the study of pressure point theory in the West. Both groups proceed from the fundamental assumption that fighting forms contain far more sophisticated and lethal meanings than mere punches and kicks. Both believe that the key to truly understanding the forms lies in having an appreciation of the principles at play in acupuncture theory and practice. And both subscribe to the tenet that it is vital to know how to heal as well as to harm. At the conclusion of the visit the Temple, the delegation was invited to return again, and Shi De Jing expressed an interest in coming to the United States in the future.

The monks themselves, many of whom have been at the Temple since childhood, give up their personal possessions and dedicate themselves entirely to the study of either or both of the twin pillars of Shaolin: Buddhism and the martial arts. Some remain at the Temple, while others depart after a time as missionaries, occasionally establishing new temples wherever their travels lead them. The gentleness of their demeanor belies the ferocity of their techniques, and in their movements, the careful observer can catch glimpses of the entire history of the martial arts. In addition to these living legends, literally thousands of other martial artists may be seen working out in the Temple and surrounding areas at any given time. One observer described it as, "martial arts heaven."

Just outside the Temple gates lies the Pagoda Forest, a group of stone monuments honoring the past masters of the Temple. The visitors climbed part way up Songshan Mountain to visit Bodhidharma's cave, where, legend has it, the Indian monk meditated for nine years before being granted entry into the Shaolin Temple. It is said that so intense was his meditation that his image was forever engraved on the rock face. A few members of this group of visitors to the Temple made the climb in order to earn the privilege of meditating on that very spot.

The term "Traditional Chinese Medicine" ("TCM") encompasses a range of time-honored medical practices—including acupuncture, herbal remedies, cupping and massage—which were developed in China over several thousand years. While such techniques are viewed as "alternative" modalities of treatment in the United States, they continue to form an integral part of China's modern health care system. Beijing's Tongren Hospital is one of the largest institutions to offer care and training in TCM.

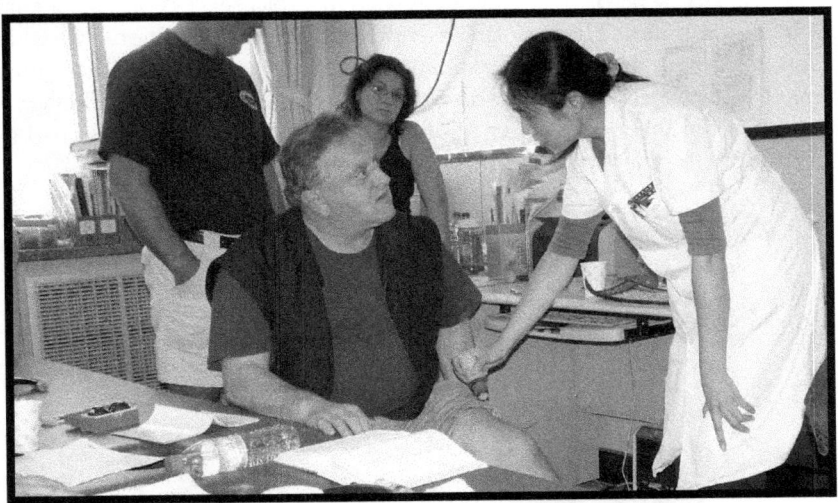

During their visit to China, George Dillman and the members of his group attended a three-day course in TCM at Tongren Hospital, taught by Dr. Ying Shou and other experts in this field. Several television and newspapers covered this event. Again, it was surprising to note the consonance of the fundamental theories underlying both the healing and the harming arts. At the conclusion of their studies, the participants were all awarded certificates.

The palace compound that stands in the heart of modern day Beijing, protected by both moat and wall is known as: "Gu Gong—The Forbidden City." Given that this was the imperial palace during the mid-Ming and the Qing Dynasties, it is not difficult to appreciate why it was considered, "forbidden." Nearby is Tiananmen Square and to the southeast lies the Temple of Heaven. In addition to the priceless treasures of all kinds on display in these vast complexes, the visitors were able to observe the inhabitants practicing T'ai Chi with fans and playing traditional musical instruments. They even had an opportunity to practice some of their own forms in this most ancient of kingdoms.

The Great Wall of China is the longest man-made structure in the world, stretching almost 4,000 miles along the border with Mongolia, from the Shanhai Pass to Lop Nur. It is visible from space. It has been built, fortified and re-built over twenty centuries, and was used by the indigenous people as a defense against the Huns, the Mongols and the Turks among others. Along the Wall watchtowers are positioned at regular intervals, allowing smoke signals to be passed along in amazingly rapid succession, like a chain of falling dominos. There is also a system of fallback positions, to which defenders could retreat if overwhelmed. The stairways of these structures were intentionally designed to confuse would-be attackers. In addition to witnessing the sheer magnificence of this wonder, the visitors again had the opportunity to practice their techniques at this extraordinary location.

In the spring of 1974, local farmers drilling for water near Xi'an stumbled across the burial site of the Terra Cotta warriors. This army of 8,000 life-sized clay soldiers and horses was interred near the necropolis of the first Emperor in 210 B.C. Each held a real weapon, probably used in actual warfare at some point in history. Within Qin Shi Huang's tomb itself the remains of many of the craftsmen who constructed it can be found. It is believed they were buried alive after completing their work so as to protect the secrets of the Emperor's tomb!

George Dillman and his senior instructors concluded their tour of China by teaching a class at the local school of one of his own students. Two special guests—senior masters of the martial arts who were visiting from Japan—were also in attendance. At this special seminar, the ancient fighting arts of Japan, China and Okinawa came together, and for the multi-national group that was privileged to be in attendance, it was a little like returning the arts that migrated from these ancient lands over the centuries and millennia, to their source.

It should also be noted that a contingent from George Dillman's association has returned to the Shaolin Temple many times after this initial visit, in order to ensure that ties between his organization and the source from which it once sprang remain strong.

Ryūkyū Kempo

In time, all things return to the source.
                                                    —The Master

CHAPTER TWENTY-THREE:
Humanity, Healing & Health

The power of Ryūkyū Kempo to inflict devastating harm on opponents is well established. But there is also a compelling case to be made that it is also one of the most *humane* methods of self-defense. When compared with the fighting methods of purely impact-based arts, like boxing for example, or the hazards of being involved in a street-fight, the benefits of being able to stun or knock out an opponent using only the lightest of touches, are readily apparent.

In terms of the risks associated with practicing pressure point techniques in the region of the head or neck, George Dillman has this to say:

> Some people say that they don't like to practice striking pressure points near the head and neck because they are worried about doing. Well with every martial art, there is a risk of harm, and we have never had a serious injury in all the years I've been doing this, in part because I make sure that all my senior people know how to heal as well as hurt.
>
> But it is incorrect to think that striking body points is so much safer than head and neck points, because when you strike a body point, the energy goes directly to the organs. I am careful about what techniques I teach to who, and when. I base a lot of that on watching to see what the student picks up.
>
> Some people are intelligent and pick things up quickly and others just don't get it—they still wouldn't even know how to bend a wrist. When they show me that they can understand how to do the technique and respect the power of that technique, then they may be ready to move on to the next level.

> Finally, it is only responsible to learn the basics of energy restoration and healing prior to practicing any pressure point techniques.
> —GMGD

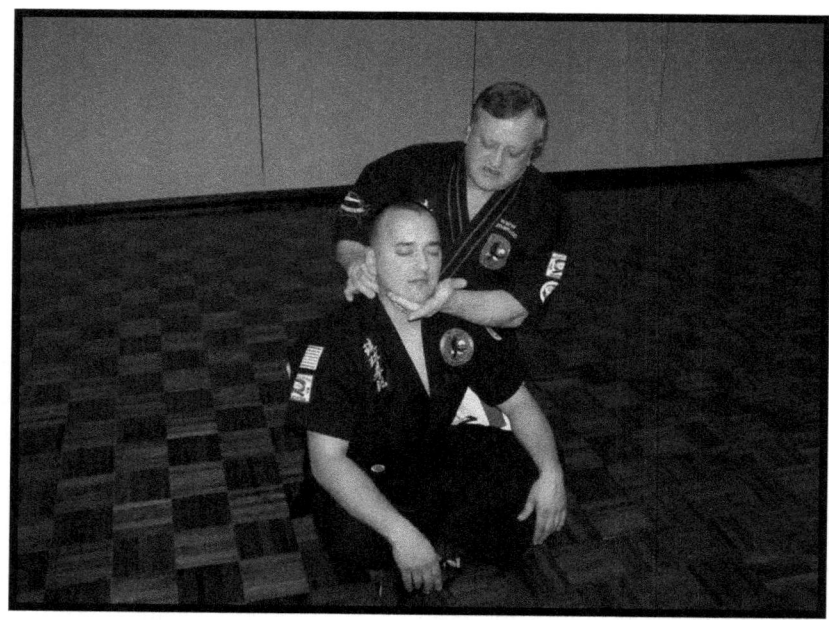

In addition to minimizing the risk of doing damage to oneself and others, there is a venerable tradition in the martial arts of linking the practices of harming and healing. With its wholesale adoption of acupuncture theory and practice, Ryūkyū Kempo's is perhaps the most complete expression of the fusion of these seemingly antithetical pursuits.

> As important as knowing how to use pressure points to hurt is knowing how to use them to heal. And not just healing others, but keeping yourself in good shape as well. I massage certain points every morning, like Stomach 36 and 37. They're at the end of the shinbone at the start of the calf muscle. I sit at the end of the bed every morning and massage those points, both sides. Stomach 36 is the golden point. I learned from a Chinese acupuncturist that whatever other point you using for healing, Stomach 36 will prevent the illness from coming back. The angle and direction for that point is in and down. You need to massage it three times, and the sickness won't return. In some acupuncture schools they teach that rubbing Stomach 36 every morning is the equivalent of getting a 'flu shot.

Other points I massage for general health include:

♦ Liver 1 and 2—Liver is the "mother" organ to the heart and it is also a "single" organ so I want to keep it healthy. I massage these points almost every day.

♦ Kidney 1—This helps to keep energy flowing. Along with Bladder 4, it also helps keep the feet and ankles strong, with good circulation. The heart has the hardest time pumping to the feet. If you look at a weight-lifter's ankles and feet, they are often very white.

♦ Stomach 37—This point is also important for the appendix. It helps keep the energy flowing through and helps keep the appendix clean.

♦ Triple Yin—I rub hard on the inside of both shins at the Triple Yin point. Then while standing I smack up and down the outsides of my legs and then smack the bottom of my feet (use a hammer fist and lightly hit the heel).When done, I massage of Kidney 1.

♦ Kidney 27—This point is very important to rub and massage. This area should be soft to the feel; if it hardens up then energy is becoming blocking up.

♦ Lung Points generally—For general health, massage the muscle area of the forearm.

♦ At nighttime I massage the Gall Bladder and Bladder points, which help you to sleep.

♦ On the back, if you feel any lumps, that indicates water (Bladder) energy backing up. These types of blockages must be massaged away otherwise they can affect the heart because water puts out fire. The direction of that type of massage is up to keep the energy going.

—GMGD

What a man can do, he ought also be able to **undo**...
—The Master

Ryūkyū Kempo

CHAPTER TWENTY-FOUR:
The Camp

In any lengthy journey, the traveler is likely to encounter phenomena that are both extraordinary and ephemeral from time to time. In fact, it may be their fleeting nature that makes them so special, like the flowering of the cherry blossoms or the nocturnal spectacle of the auroras. And whether their appearance is measured in minutes and hours or months and years, they are to be treasured, for they are unlikely to come again.

The Camp at Deer Lake was one such phenomenon.

Built in a clearing hacked out of the wooded slope of a hill in central Pennsylvania in 1972, it was first used as a training tool by perhaps the greatest boxer ever to have entered the ring: Muhammad Ali. Over the years that followed, a veritable parade of fighting legends came to commune in this special place, each leaving his name emblazoned on one of the massive boulders that guided the way up the winding path.

A quarter of a century later, the Camp changed hands, passing to George Dillman, who, after all, had been there from the beginning. This special place became a nexus—a physical and notional focal point for senior Ryūkyū Kempo practitioners all around the world—and for those who were fortunate enough to travel and train there, in the clean mountain air, at the feet of the masters, it was an experience they will always treasure.

> I was at the Deer Lake campsite with Ali before there was anything there. We came up the hill in Jeeps when it was just woods, and Ali said, "we're going to build this here; we're going to build that there," and I didn't see it—all I saw was a mountain. Then in came the contractors and sure enough it came to life. That's one of the reasons why I have a real fondness for this place. In 1980 Ali was looking to retire and first talked to me about me buying the Camp.
>
> We were sitting on the stoop talking about getting older, and he said, "why don't you buy the Camp? I'd like to see you have it and I'll make you an offer you can't refuse!" I didn't have the money at the time—I couldn't even have afforded the upkeep, I mean the place had eighteen buildings! And that's when Ali told me that I should think about running camps for martial artists. I didn't think anyone would be interested at the time.
>
> By the 1990s, I was teaching pressure point seminars, and sometimes thought, "boy this seminar idea could work now, if only Ali's offer was still good…" Well one day in 1997 I was out in the Midwest doing a seminar and a friend called to tell me that the Camp was up for sale." I called the real estate office right away and put in an offer at the same price that Ali had offered me in 1980. The agent called me back and said "no," so I told him to talk to Ali directly and tell him who the offer came from, and that I would cover the expenses of the sale. He called me back the next day and told me the offer was accepted. I was shocked. The agent said, "of all the people who could buy this camp, I would want George to have it."
>
> So I ended up owning the Camp. It had been empty for a seven years and was kind of in a state of disrepair, but a bunch of volunteers—thirty or more—from as far as Chicago came in and helped me remodel it. They helped me clean and paint and fix and I fed and housed them and taught a special seminar for them. Some young ladies from Peoria came in and cleaned and treated the boulders that are painted with the names of all the

famous fighters who trained at this camp. I sank three or four times the purchase price into renovations—new roofs, ceilings, plumbing, carpeting. Since then it has become a place where martial artists from all different systems and styles come to learn, to teach, to share and to research.

Some people have come and gone over the years, and all I have to say about that is, there's givers and there's takers. Some people came in to me and pretended to be loyal, but were secretly planning to take what they could get and leave to start their own organizations. For some people it's all about money. I've never given away anything for money. I've always taught good, solid, clean martial arts. If you look back in history, you'll read about how Choki Motobu would not accept payment for teaching the martial arts, but every day on his doorstep would appear bags and bags of groceries. His students knew he had to eat, and they made sure he was provided for. Things have become much more commercial now. It wasn't that way back when I first started training.

For those who have endured, though, the adventure continues. Some of the things we've been working on over the years are pretty much perfected. Others are still in the research and development phase...

—GMGD

When you encounter a special person, place, or thing, enjoy every moment, for it will be gone in the blink of an eye.

—The Master

CHAPTER TWENTY-FIVE:
The Science

Dr. Ralph Buschbacher has been studying Ryūkyū Kempo since the early 1970s. He attended the University of Virginia for college and medical school. During this time he ran the biggest independent karate group at the University. He continued to train with George Dillman and travelled back to the home school in Reading many weekends. He also hosted multiple seminars in Virginia. Dr. Buschbacher earned his fourth degree black belt around the same time he earned his medical doctorate. He says that both degrees were equally important to him.

Dr. Buschbacher and George Dillman spent a lot of time talking about the medical and neurological aspects of many self-defense techniques involving pressure points. In fact Buschbacher gave Dillman his first anatomy book. According to Buschbacher, "it wasn't a lay person's book. It was a dissection book, the kind professionals in medicine use." He also gave Dillman several other medical texts over the years. He notes: "Dillman was very good at reading them and was obviously a great student of anatomy and physiology."

Dr. Buschbacher explained to Dillman how reflexes, the Golgi tendon (which contributes to the stretch reflex of muscles), and intrafusal and extrafusal muscle fibers worked. Dillman was even invited into the cadaver room and got to see everything first hand. Dr. Buschbacher said, "he loved it. He was like a kid in a candy store. He loved seeing how tendons worked. We examined how things are interconnected and how nerves travel." From this experience, Dillman started thinking about a three-dimensional way of looking at the body. Instead of just thinking, "okay, here is the surface. I'm going to hit it as hard as I can," he began thinking, "what am I putting that energy into?"

Ryūkyū Kempo

Dillman visited the anatomy lab several times. He and Buschbacher spent most of their time on the arm and neck areas. One of their studies involved the positioning of the arm during a punch. There is a membrane that connects the radius and the ulna called the "interosseous membrane." By examining the arm of a cadaver in different positions, it became evident that this membrane is taut in the three-quarters position and folds over on itself in a full-twist position. As a result, the three-quarter punch provides more support and allows transfer of energy from the strong distal part of radius to the strong proximal part of the ulna. Dr. Buschbacher's findings in this regard were subsequently published. (See Buschbacher R.M., Coplin B., Buschbacher L., PROPER PUNCHING TECHNIQUE IN THE MARTIAL ARTS, *Arch. Phys. Med. Rehabil.* 1992; 73:1019).

Over the course of their association, Dr. Buschbacher shared many other correlations between medicine and the martial arts with Dillman, and even helped to teach martial arts seminars in the United States and Germany. For example, he explained how the rub-point on the back of the elbow works medically by stimulating reflexes in the body, and how to attack underneath the rib to get at the pressure points where the nerves run, and he showed the best location, angle, and direction to strike in order to break a rib.

> ### Dr. Charles Terry
>
> Grandmaster Dillman has been teaching anatomy and physiology in his classes and seminars since before I was in medical school. There is no doubt that this had a significant influence on my decision to study medicine. The image of a great martial arts master whose ability to injure is matched with an equal ability to heal, is entrenched in martial arts folklore. This begins with a basic understanding of how the body works. It is not coincidence that this influence drew both myself and Dr. Buschbacher to the field of Physical Medicine and Rehabilitation.
>
> Dillman has always referred to his time with Dr. Buschbacher with great pride. Before learning anything about the science of the martial arts, Dillman developed his skills to a high level. He was not satisfied with just knowing how to do something, but he always sought to understand why a technique or theory works. It is clear the time he spent studying cadavers and medical books with the assistance of Dr. Buschbacher has helped to add depth to his seminar presentations. It has also enhanced his performance of many techniques.
>
> When Dillman started working with pressure points and knockout techniques he was quick to seek input from the physicians in his organization. By combining acupuncture theory with a solid understanding of western anatomy and physiology, he has been able to make remarkable strides with the science of self-defense.

Dr. Charles Terry did his residency in Physical Medicine and Rehabilitation at the Hospital of the University of Pennsylvania. He had several discussions about pressure point theory with Dr. Mark Stecker, a prominent Neurologist, which led them to arrange a joint study between the Department of Neurology and the Department of Rehabilitation Medicine.

Professor Dillman had many seminars in the Philadelphia area, and they were able to coordinate a study with the physicians, a team of technicians, and some of Dillman's top students from around the country. Because of the size and amount of medical equipment used, the study was done in the Physical Therapy department at the hospital.

Dr. Terry explains the purpose of the study as an effort to "evaluate physiologic changes occurring during knockout techniques." Twelve healthy volunteers participated in the study. Martial artists performed various pressure point knockout techniques on the volunteers while the physicians monitored different parameters. The volunteers were hooked up to an electrocardiogram monitor (EKG), and an electroencephalogram (EEG), as well as blood pressure, heart rate, and oxygen saturation monitors.

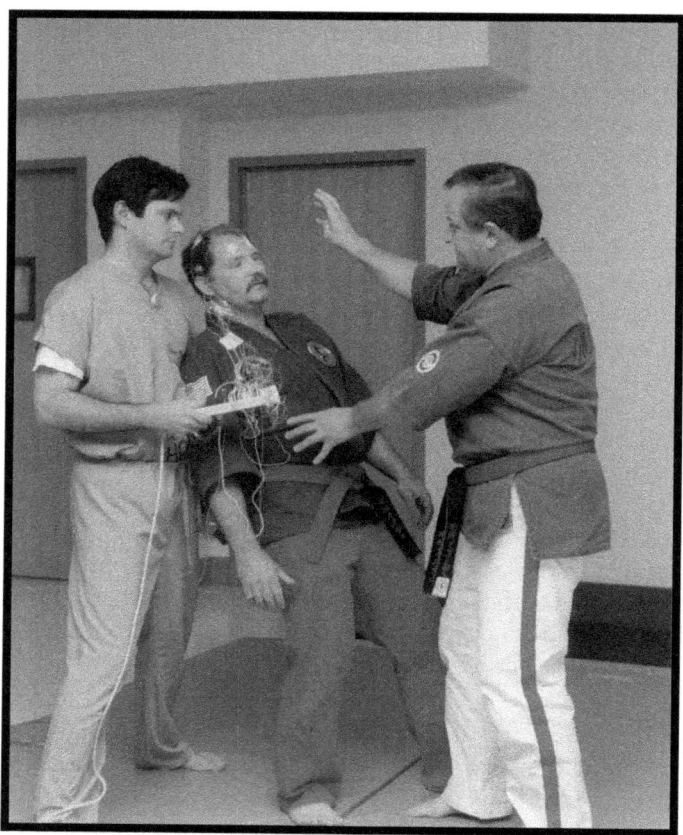

The physicians agreed that pressure point techniques clearly can produce short periods of altered responsiveness. With respect to Western Medicine, the mechanism for the knockout effect was less clear. There were some technical difficulties with artifact (spurious observation or result arising from preparatory or investigative procedures) occurring in the parameters monitored due to the motion of the volunteer during the knockout strike. There was also some difficulty keeping wires in place, so the martial artists had to choose techniques which would minimize the movement of the volunteer.

A mild elevation in mean blood pressure before the knockouts was observed. There was a small, but not significant, trend toward slightly higher blood pressure immediately after the knockouts. There were no significant changes in diastolic blood pressure, heart rate, or oxygen saturation. The high degree of artifact with EEG recordings limited the ability of the scientists to perform quantitative analysis. There was no evidence of seizure activity or cardiac arrhythmias.

Each subject was given two words to recall at the appearance of unresponsiveness and later asked to recall the two words. Brief neurological exams were performed after the knockouts. Ten subjects were knocked out while standing and two were seated during the testing. The estimated period of unresponsiveness varied from eleven to fifty-five seconds. Despite being immobile and unresponsive, subjects were able to remember both words in three of the twelve knockouts and recalled one word in two of the twelve knockouts.

There were many conclusions from the study. The scientists agreed that pressure point techniques can produce short periods of altered responsiveness. The mechanism that produced these results, however, remains uncertain. There are several possible explanations:

◆ There may be reflex inhibition of limb muscle activity such as that seen in cataplexy (although the EEGs did not fully support this theory). Future study with recordings of electromyographic (EMG) activity may be helpful.

◆ Another possibility is that where the techniques result in "an issociated state of consciousness," the effect may be primarily psychological. This possibility was neither confirmed nor refuted by the study.

◆ The possibility that volunteers were just "cooperating" with the martial artists was also discussed by the scientists and rejected, based at least in part on the participants' expressed desire to determine the scientific basis of the physiological results.

◆ One important conclusion of the study was that there was no evidence that pressure point techniques result in immediately dangerous physical effects such as arrythmias, seizures, desaturation, or syncope. This study was published in 1999 (See Terry C., Barclay D.K., Patterson T., *et al.*, PHYSIOLOGIC STUDY OF PRESSURE POINT TECHNIQUES USED IN THE

Ryūkyū Kempo

MARTIAL ARTS, *J. Sports Med. Phys. Fitness*, 1999; 39:328-35). It was also written up in *Black Belt* magazine by Chris Thomas.

> ### Dr. Charles Terry's Comments
>
> It was great to be able to set up this study. I managed to be in just the right place at the right time. Grandmaster Dillman encouraged some of his best students to participate. Members of DKI have always been inquisitive and all seemed genuinely interested in analyzing their techniques from a medical and scientific perspective.
>
> My medical colleagues were enthusiastic about studying the physiologic effects of pressure point techniques. Before and after the study, we had discussions about potential medical uses for pressure point techniques. Some thoughts included using pressure points for the treatment of insomnia, as well as for anesthesia during surgery and for pain management in the peri-operative period.
>
> During the actual study, we had some difficulty with motion artifact and wires coming loose. Doing knockouts with the volunteers seated helped with this somewhat. It would be very interesting to do a similar study with "no-touch" knockouts. A study with "no-touch" knockouts and wireless equipment might prove even more useful.
>
> From a personal standpoint, as a martial artist, and more recently as a physician, I've had some concerns about the safety of knockout techniques. This study helped to put me at ease. Some practitioners have claimed to "stop the heart" or "turn off the lungs" during a knockout. This would be incredibly unsafe from a medical standpoint and was not demonstrated during any of the knockouts studied. There appeared to be no short-term negative health issues related to doing pressure point knockouts. The long-term effects of these techniques remains to be studied.

In 2002, another clinical trial was conducted in Indianapolis, Indiana with a well-known surgeon named Dr. Robert Joseph. In the University of Pennsylvania study the subjects were wired up to the computers, and the wires interfered with the test result to some degree. In Indianapolis, all the equipment was wireless.

Dr. Joseph put together a study with eight subjects. All subjects were monitored with for Heart Rate, Respiratory Rate, Blood Pressure, EKG, and Bispectral Index (BIS). BIS is an electroencephalogram (EEG) based index which looks at the frequency and amplitude of brain waves. It was initially developed to monitor the depth of anesthesia. Deeper anesthesia increases the amplitude of the EEG waves and lowers the frequency.

In this study, there were no statistically significant changes in heart rate or blood pressure in the subjects. There was a statistically significant decrease in the BIS, but for the most part this change was not a great as that seen with deep anesthesia. All subjects briefly stopped breathing. One stopped breathing for longer than sixty seconds, but this subject was later determined to have sleep apnea syndrome.

Dr. Charles Terry's Comments

This study had fewer participants than the University of Pennsylvania study (eight as opposed to twelve), but was able to eliminate some of the interference caused by having too many wires attached to the subjects. Neither study found significant changes in blood pressure or heart rate. The observation of apnea (stopped breathing) in the Indiana study is quite interesting from a medical standpoint. It suggests that perhaps knockout techniques should not be performed on students with sleep apnea or other significant breathing problems.

As we learn more about the physiologic effects of pressure point techniques it should be possible to further narrow the range of "safe" test subjects. It would be prudent to have all knockout volunteers undergo a brief medical history prior to being knocked out.

Again, it is likely that different knockout techniques actually work by different mechanisms. Further study is clearly needed to determine how different subjects respond to the same knockout technique and, conversely, how one subject responds to several different knockout techniques.

Epiphany

When I started to see the light, I called a meeting of the senior instructors in Virginia and taught a special seminar for them. And I opened up with the statement: "There's no blocks in any katas." They thought I was kidding at first. So I proceeded to demonstrate! And this wasn't just "a block can be a punch and a punch can be a block depending on how hard you hit." This was something entirely new. Moves toward your own body—which we had been taught were "getting ready" moves—

those were the real blocks. What we had learned as blocks were actually something totally different. More often than not they were pressure point strikes.

But even after I discovered pressure points, I didn't regret the time I spent practicing martial arts without knowing about them. That is because the pressure points are like the warheads, but you still need a delivery system, and that would be your conventional punching and kicking. You still need timing, rhythm and coordination. Without the ability to get the weapon to the target, all you have is book knowledge.

—GMGD

Dr. Charles Terry's Comments

I have always been impressed with Grandmaster Dillman's desire to study medically and to develop scientific support for the Dillman Theory. From the early days with Dr. Ralph Buschbacher, he was able to support the three-quarters punch anatomically. It is more useful than a full-twist punch for striking a single rib, striking the solar plexus, and striking many pressure points on the body. The connection of the interosseus membrane between the radius and the ulna clearly adds structural support to the forearm during a three-quarter punch.

In science, increasing or decreasing surface area often has a significant impact on a chemical or physical reaction. This holds true when comparing a punch to a slap. A punch has more penetrating force. Professor Dillman has long taught students to punch with only the first two knuckles (actually the second and third proximal interphylangeal joints). This is useful for several reasons:

- It concentrates the most energy into an area of about one-square inch which will cause more damage/pain to an attacker.

- These joints are supported in a straight line with the radius and the ulna which decreases the risk of wrist injury during punching.

- It also prevents the diversion of energy into excessive wrist movement. These joints are stronger than the fourth and fifth interphylangeal joints. In fact, a common injury known as a "boxer's fracture" can occur when someone punches and makes contact with the fifth knuckle.

Professor Dillman teaches keep the thumb straight while doing a shuto.

- This prevents being countered with a thumb lock.

- It also allows the tip of the thumb to be used to strike several areas of the body such as the ulnar nerve near the elbow, or the carotid artery in the neck.

- And keeping the hand in a more vertical position when striking with the ulnar side of a shuto allows for more effective striking of the carotid artery near the anterior border of the sterno-cleido-mastoid (SCM) muscle.

As far as what is actually happening during a pressure point knockout, I believe different knockouts work for different reasons. Some are clearly vascular, such as striking the carotid artery. The brain is enclosed within the fixed volume of the skull. Therefore, there is a special mechanism by which the blood pressure to the brain is controlled. The carotid body is a cluster of receptors in the neck (near the acupuncture point Stomach 9) that decreases the blood flow to the brain when stimulated. This leads to any easy knockout.

However, anyone with a family or personal history of strokes, aneurysms, or atherosclerosis is at increased risk of having a stroke if struck in this spot. Therefore, Stomach 9 should not be struck repeatedly in practice, particularly in anyone with increased risk. In fact, simply massaging this point can affect the heart rate and decrease blood flow to the head resulting in a knockout.

Other knockouts may be concussive. Striking points on the jaw (Stomach 5), forehead (Gallbladder 13, 14, 15), or the back of the head (Gallbladder 12, 20) may lead to unconsciousness by causing a mild concussion. Strikes to the arm or leg, may cause a whiplash kind of effect on the skull. This may result in unconsciousness through activation of the vascular system in the neck and/or a concussive effect.

Some strikes to the body or combination strikes to multiple targets may result in an overload of the nervous system. Often when the body is overloaded with stimuli it responds by shutting down. It is possible that activation of several peripheral nerves sends an overload of signals to the central nervous system.

Tendons and the surface of bones are quite sensitive to pain. Rubbing or striking these areas will send pain signals to the central nervous system via nerves in the skin as well as the underlying structures.

There are several reflexes in the body that can be utilized for self-defense purposes. When a physician strikes the knee (patellar tendon), the leg reflexively kicks out. This is similar to striking the triceps tendon (Triple Warmer 11). These reflexes can be found on many different parts of the body and can help trigger a predictable physiologic response in any attacker. The crossed-extensor reflex involves stimulating one limb and activating a reflex through the spinal cord in one or more other limbs. When you touch a hot stove with your right hand, your right arm will reflexively retract. Without involvement of the brain, a reflex arc in the spinal cord will nearly simultaneously cause the left knee to bend. This results in more quickly pulling your hand away from the painful stimulus.

CHAPTER TWENTY-SIX:
The Master Class

Congratulations! And welcome. For those who have endured to this point, you have now graduated to **the Master Class** (which is honored to share its name with the excellent web presence of the same name hosted by Grandmaster Chris Thomas). And now, the time has come at last to present the rest of the story:

Those of you already familiar with the story so far may recall that in 1988, George Dillman visited Japan in order to explore firsthand the culture from which the arts he loves so dearly arose.

It was during this pilgrimage, that three revelatory events took place:

- Dillman was able to view the complete *Bubishi*.

- Dillman received an extraordinary gift from *Ichiro Ohba*.

- Dillman visited the *Reiki* school in Gifu.

To hear Dillman tell it, each of these events was to have a powerful effect on his practice of the martial arts, in many ways as profound as the time he spent with *Hohan Soken* in the 1970s. Moreover, like his initial introduction to pressure points by the Okinawan master half a century ago, the effects of these events took many years to come to fruition—a cognitive "delayed touch" if you will—in that it was not until his retirement from active teaching that he truly came to grips with them, translating dusty texts, cross-referencing pressure point charts, and combing through decades of study and practice to formulate and present the theories that follow.

一是金勢
人懷難用長棍、故取
冷手監穿國外須用
棍根進步打手最疾、

I. THE BIBLE OF THE MARTIAL ARTS [武備志]

Most serious martial artist are familiar with the Bubishi, also known as "the Bible of Karate." In its modern incarnation, it is a volume of a few hundred pages focusing primarily on the Okinawan open-handed arts. Various excellent translations of this important material are widely available wherever books are sold.

What fewer practitioners appreciate, however, is that this well-known text is a highly abbreviated version of one small part of the Chinese original: Mao Yuanyi's seventeenth century compendium: *Wubei Zhi: Treatise on Armament Technology*.

Consisting of over *ten thousand pages*, divided into *two hundred and forty chapters*, in over *one hundred* volumes, the original work is the most comprehensive written treatment of martial practices in recorded history.

It is this complete encyclopedia of all things martial which George Dillman was privileged to view during his time in the Far East, and, given his photographic memory, the multitude of secrets contained therein undoubtedly helped to shape his understanding of this field of study.

懸腳虛餌彼輕進、
換腿決不饒輕趕上
一掌滿天星誰敢再
來比竝、
丘劉勢左搬右掌劈
來腳入步連心挪更
拳法探馬均打人一
着命盡、

THE ORIGINAL *BUBISHI*

While we were there, we were invited to visit a six-hundred plus year old *ninja* castle—the last remaining authentic one, I believe. And in one room, they had the entire <u>Bubishi</u> laid out. Volume after volume. It's not just about certain martial arts—it's about everything! It's the martial arts encyclopedia. It tells you all kinds of things. It tell you how to shoot a bow. It even tells you how to *make* a bow! It tells you how to make a sword, how to sharpen a sword, and how to use a sword. There's an entire volume just on hand weapons. I got to look it over and I filmed it all.

—GMGD

脚踹上弩圖

坦腹势

坦腹势者、即坦腹刺也、法能冲刺中殺進、如崩山右脚右手蒼龍出水势、向前進步腰擊者法、

II. The *Ohba*–Yūjin Study

On this same trip, Dillman spent a week as the live-in guest of a local attorney—*Ichiro Ohba*—in Gifu, thanks to an introduction from an embassy official. While Ohba was not himself a martial artist, there had been many in his family, and, after a period of evaluation, he saw fit to entrust Dillman with a prized-possession—a multi-volume study of various martial arts that had been in his family for decades.

The study of the martial arts is truly the journey of a lifetime, and George Dillman's recent path illustrates this truth perfectly, because it was not until *after* his retirement that he had the time and resources to complete the translation and analysis of the aforementioned study. And what he discovered in this precious time capsule was truly astonishing—not just because of the information contained in the *printed* materials, but also as a result of the insights gleaned from copious *hand-written notes* scattered throughout. Ohba never revealed the identity of the scribe, but his (or her) deep understanding of a variety of pivotal martial concepts is immediately apparent. Moving forward, let's just call the unknown writer, "*Yūjin*."[6]

---

[6] "Our friend" (友人).

Ichiro Ohba

I asked a contact at the embassy to get me an introduction to anyone who had knowledge of pressure points. They introduced me to *Ichiro Ohba*, who was the District Attorney for Gifu. He wasn't a martial artist himself, but there had been several in his family. I stayed with him for a week, and during that time, he asked me to teach my method to his son, and he watched what I was doing. I think he was testing me in a way.

—GMGD

Ryūkyū Kempo

III. First Principles [原則]

Around the time of this writing, *Black Belt Magazine* published an article underscoring the importance of martial principles and comparing and contrasting those of some of the most influential masters of the Twentieth Century (including George Dillman). Given the age and pedigree of the *Ohba-Yūjin* study, it should come as no surprise that these notes also emphasize the importance of the philosophical and strategic underpinnings of techniques and tactics. Specific precepts enunciated therein include the following:

- You must come to the arts with a clear and open mind.
- The most important aspect of the journey is cultivating the warrior spirit.
- Take your time—after all, it is *your* journey.
- Focus on one thing at a time and start small.
- Study the basics assiduously (for it is here that the true secrets are found).
- Do not get in your own way.
- Follow the path of harmony.
- Accept guidance with humility and gratitude.
- Seek the truth within.
- Conduct yourself as a gentleman (or lady).

George Dillman's Nine Principles

1. Be resolved to defend yourself.
2. If you wish to attack West, first attack East.
3. Make your self-defense response a conscious decision.
4. The best self-defense is awareness and avoidance.
5. Your voice is a weapon.
6. Act first, act decisively.
7. Never surrender advantage.
8. Face your attacker.
9. Take action at the first sign of a threat.

As important as martial principles themselves—which generally deal with such concepts as taking the initiative; duality/multiplicity; mental and spiritual strength; creativity and adaptability; individuality; persistence; and awareness of the environment—is the understanding that *whatever* they may be, they are a necessary part of our studies.

Without certain cerebral components, physical technique is just brawling. And without some kind of moral compass as a guide, even the most effective fighter is missing the bigger picture. The mental and spiritual pieces don't just help to complete the martial puzzle—in many ways, they *are* the puzzle. Consider this: With a little luck and a modicum of awareness, the average person may be fortunate enough never to have to use the martial arts to defend himself, but *no one* can navigate life without calling on certain principles as a guide on a regular basis.

FUNAKOSHI'S *NIJUKUN*
Begin and end with respect;
There is no first strike in karate;
Karate is an aid to justice;
First know self, then others;
Spirit first, technique second;
Set your mind free;
Misfortune laziness/accidents;
Karate training not only in dojo;
Entire life to learn karate;
Karate in daily life → secrets;
Karate is like boiling water;
Do not think that you have to win – rather that you do not have to lose;
Make adjustments according to your opponent;
The outcome of the battle depends on how you handle weakness and strength;
Think of hands and feet as swords;
When you leave home, there are a million enemies waiting for you;
Beginners master low stances; natural body positions are for advanced students;
Practice sets exactly; actual combat is another matter;
Withdrawal of power, extension/contraction; swift/leisurely technique;
Be mindful, diligent, and resourceful, in your pursuit of karatedo.

FONG'S TEN COMMANDS
The ultimate is within you;
Spirit before mind before body
Practice makes reflexive;
Await to attack at right moment;
Attack from the void;
Defend with control;
Listen to your opponent;
Don't try to drive the situation…
Win or *learn*;
Know when to walk away;

EIGHT LEE PRECEPTS
Be like water;
Use no way as way;
Be/express/faith in yourself;
There is but one family;
Practical dreamer back by action;
Change with change is changeless;
Absorb what is useful;
Walk on!

DILLMAN'S NINE RULES
Be resolved to defend yourself;
To attack west, first attack east;
Self-defense conscious decision;
Best self-defense aware/avoid
Your voice is a weapon;
Act first, act decisively;
Never surrender advantage;
Face your attacker;
Take action at first sign of threat;

KANO'S FIVE PRINCIPLES
Observe self, others, environment;
Seize initiative in any undertaking;
Consider fully, act decisively;
Know when to stop;
Keep to the middle;

FIVE UESHIBA MAXIMS
Extend your mind;
Know your partner's mind;
Respect your partner's *ki*;
Put self in partner's place;
Perform with confidence;

A. INITIATIVE
B. DUALITY/MULTIPLICITY
C. MENTAL/SPIRITUAL
D. INDIVIDUALITY
E. FLEXIBILITY/ADAPTABILITY
F. PERSISTENCE/DETERMINATION
G. ENVIRONMENT/SURROUNDINGS

IV. INITIAL STEPS FORWARD (AND BACK) [前進後退]

Yūjin—and many other masters besides—stress that karate is a *complete* art, designed over the centuries to defend against *any* kind of attack. Like many other Japanese arts, it is also exquisitely, intricately, and carefully crafted. Accordingly, it should come as no surprise that its first lessons are among the most important ones.

Even though many styles of karate incorporate a degree of ground grappling, it is primarily a 'stand-up' fighting system. As a result, the majority of its armamentarium is most commonly employed to best effect in a vertical posture. Being taken down by an opponent skilled in groundwork, therefore, presents significant limitations, and is to be avoided in most cases.

Appropriately enough, the first few moves of the I-pattern form commonly taught to beginners *(Taikyoku Shodan)* clearly illlustrate defenses to this very method of attack.

STAND UP!

The basic moves needed to keep from being taken down are right there at the start of *Taikyoiku Shodan*. The attacker needs to close with you to get the job done, and you can't help but see the head grab and turn in those first few moves. More lethal techniques to deal with this are contained in the higher level forms like *Naihanchi* and *Passai*, but your attacker probably won't ever get up again if you use these...

—GMGD

STAY UP!

There is a counter for everything. I remember visiting a jujitsu school with Ohba, where the owner invited me to demonstrate my art. Every lock these guys tried—and they were damn good—I was able to counter. At the end of the visit, he presented me with a uniform for his school. I think that was what impressed Ohba the most, because he knew how good these guys were. There are certain moves that will reliably work to get you out of a grappling situation. One of my personal favorites is the foot-to-hand move in *Passai*—works every time!

—GMGD

V. Sanchin [三戦] and Tensho [転掌]

Prominently featured in the *Ohba-Yūjin* notes are references to the importance of practicing two particular *kata*: *Tensho* and *Sanchin*. Together, these twin forms teach the practitioner both the 'hard' and 'soft' aspects of the art.

- *Sanchin* (三戦 "Three Battles"): With its pigeon-toed stance, dynamic tension-induced body-armor, and three simple striking weapons (punch, spear hand, palm heel), the 'hard' elements of *Sanchin* are readily apparent in this form.

- *Tensho* (転掌 "Revolving Hands"): By contrast the continuous flowing hand movements and sinuous breathing pattern of *Tensho* provide insight into the softer elements of the practice.[7]

Regardless of what form or treatise they are drawn from, there are only so many possible striking surfaces and configurations for the human hand, and, depending on which version of *Tensho* you practice, all of them may be present in this kata:

- **Regular Fist:** Two-knuckle, three-knuckle, Okinawan variations.

- **One knuckle fist:** ("Phoenix Fist").

- **Open hand:** Bottom edge ("Iron Sword Hand").

- **Open hand:** Top edge ("Iron Bone Hand").

- **Open hand/palm:** Front ("Iron Sand Palm").

- **Open hand/wrist:** Back ("Blood Pool Hand").

- **One/two finger:** ("Blade/s of Grass").

- **All fingers together:** ("Iron Spear Hand").

- **All fingers splayed:** ("Iron Claw Hand").

---

[7] *Tensho* may be a variant of the Southern Chinese Kung Fu form *Rokkishu* and also encompasses many of the movements seen in the famous White Crane form—*Hakutsuru*.

◆ **Breathing:** Also central to the practice of *Tensho* and *Sanchin* is the method of breathing. In both cases, the focus is on deep, inward, controlled breathing with corresponding muscular dynamic tension, but in *Sanchin*, this is performed in the harder *yang* style, with sharp, punctuated inhalation and exhalation, whereas in *Tensho*—like the form's hand movements—the focus is on employing the more circular, fluid, *yin* method. While these 'cousins' are both introspective relative to the rest of the *kata* 'family,' they contrast sharply in intent and execution when compared to each other.

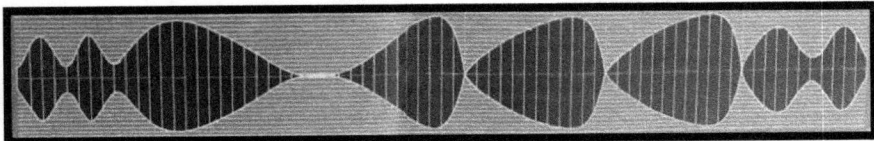

BREATHE IN, BREATHE OUT

The importance of correct breathing in these forms can't be overstated.

When you breathe in, you weaken your opponent's yin organ systems. Try this when stepping in to apply a finger lock—your opponent will drop like a rock!

But you also need to be careful when using this approach, because when you breathe in, you also weaken your own yin organ system. If you know this in advance, you can time your breathing with your strikes so you don't leave yourself open for too long.

In the same way, when you breathe out, you strengthen your own yin system, but again, you also strengthen your opponent's. This is part of why we *kiai* on certain strikes. And again, you need to apply this knowledge carefully because it works on both you and your opponent.

All of this—and much more—is contained in the breathing for those forms...

—GMGD

Ryūkyū Kempo

THREE POINTS

George Dillman has always maintained that striking a number of pressure points, either simultaneously or in series, will have an exponential effect on the opponent. Consistent with teachings in some of the ancient treatises, the progression is said to be something like this:

- One point: Will cause pain and disorientation.
- Two points: Will cause systemic dysfunction.
- Three points: Will cause unconsciousness.
- Four points: Will cause serious injury.
- Five points: Can be deadly.

Citing no less an authority than legendary Kung Fu Master Dr. Yang Jwing-Ming, Dillman states that the character 'three' in the name of the form *Sanchin* is also an allusion to the critical power of striking three points, and adds that accordingly, this *kata* can also be translated as: 'Three Points.'" As an example, he cites the way in which, with the correct method of application, the Iron Bone Hand can be used to activate ST-5, ST-9, and SI-16 all at the same time.

VI. Sanchō [山頂]

Another treasure to be unearthed in this academic excavation was the following teaching:

> *"This martial art originated from three peaks. The three peaks are Tiger Peak, Palm Peak, and Eyebrow Peak."*

In attempting to de-code this message from the past, one thought springs immediately to mind: tiger claw and palm heel are both hand weapons (and styles unto themselves). But what about the reference to: "eyebrow"?

According to Dillman, this may refer both to either (or both) a target point *and* a system. The eyebrow is a favorite middle-knuckle target in *Ryukyu Kempo*. And *Bak Mei*—also known as the White Eyebrow [8] school—is known for its use of the phoenix fist. Whatever the precise meaning of this translation, it is clear that the writer intended to convey that we should look to the proper origin points in searching for the tools of our craft.

When considering tiger claw, palm heel, and a single-digit weapon, the correlation with the six *ji* hands described in the *Bubishi* is unmistakable.

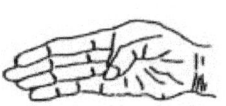
1. Iron Bone Hand.

2. Claw Hand.

3. Iron Sand Palm.

4. Blood Pool Hand.

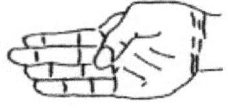
5. Sword Hand.

6. One Blade of Grass Hand.

---

[8] This ancient school is named for one of the legendary Five Elders who survived the destruction of the Shaolin Monastery during the *Qing* dynasty.

Ryūkyū Kempō

> ### A Rare Tool
>
> As anyone who has worked in the fine dining industry knows, there is a simple yet reliable way to test whether a steak has been cooked to perfection without actually puncturing it: Touching one's own thumb to each finger in order will alter the firmness of the flesh under the thumb, thereby closely approximating the feeling of a properly prepared steak at every temperature from rare to well done.

Blending lessons from several of these newly-discovered sources, it is interesting to note that touching one's thumb (earth) to each of the fingers in order (wood, fire, metal, water) produces a different hand weapon:

- **Thumb alone:** Tiger Claw, Iron Sand Palm;

- **Thumb to index finger:** Iron Sword Hand, Okinawan Fist, Phoenix Fist, Index-knuckle Fist, Single Blade of Grass, Palm Heel;

- **Thumb to middle finger:** Mantis Hand, Blood Pool Hand;

- **Thumb to ring finger:** Iron Bone Hand/Ridge Hand;

- **Thumb to little finger:** Crane Beak (actually, this is more accurately described as thumb to all four fingers, *including* the little finger).

WEAPON OF CHOICE

There is a proper tool for every job.

After so many years of putting this stuff out there, there are *still* many people who don't understand that—who haven't put in the work to drill down to the deeper levels…

♦ **Striking:** Many people have pretty much gotten this part down. Every system has striking in it, and preferred target points. And while they may not all understand *why* it works, or know the *best* way to make it work, they are mostly all on the same page at least.

With this approach, it's important to remember: The smaller the weapon, the greater the effect [in descending order of focus]:

- Whole Hand/Palm—Palm Heel, Crane Neck, Back Fist;

- Partial Hand/Palm—Knife Hand, Ridge Hand, Hammer Fist;

- Knuckles Only—Regular Fist (two/three knuckle, Okinawan);

- All Fingers—Spear Hand, Tiger Claw, Crane Beak;

- Single Knuckle/Digit—Phoenix Fist, Blade of Grass.

For example, if you strike the point just above the eye in the right place [at the 'turn' of the eyebrow], with the right tool [Phoenix Fist], the result can be devastating.

The base of the thumb is another advanced hand-tool [Iron Bone Hand]. To make all sorts of tools, turn your palm upward and shape it like a saucer holding water. The backs of the four knuckles can also be used loosely [Blood Pool Hand]. And don't forget the power of the palm, especially the base of the forefinger [Iron Sand Palm].

♦ **Rubbing/Touching:** Too many people only understand this at a basic level. It's not just on/off [oscillating]; it's about really getting down into the deep channels using leverage, and this is where hand conditioning is so important. Too many students ignore the power of pressure point touching/grabbing, as with LI-1, LU-5, and the points around the wrist [Iron Claw Hand].

Ryūkyū Kempo

SPECIAL WEAPONS— TARGETS

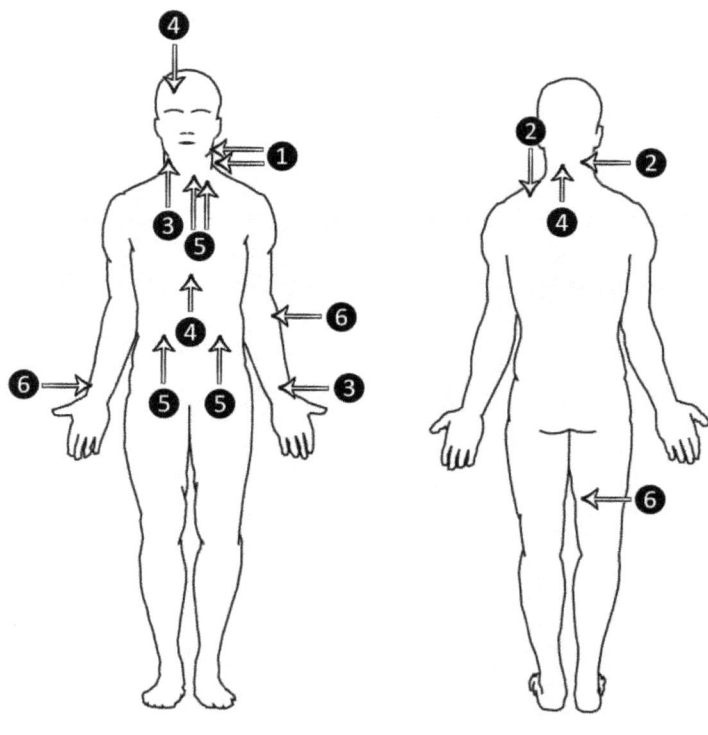

- ❶ Iron Bone Hand
- ❷ Iron Sword Hand
- ❸ Blood Pool Hand
- ❹ Iron Sand Palm
- ❺ Blade(s) of Grass
- ❻ Iron Claw Hand

> ◆ **The Mind:** In all the years I've been doing this, I have never come across *anyone* I couldn't make an instant believer out of using these physical techniques (and at the same time, I've also never accidentally injured anyone—not a bad record!). But there is another level which involves pretty advanced theoretical research. Even now, we don't fully understand it, but in order to start down this path, you need to begin by truly *believing* that there is a way to make it work, and staying *committed* to finding the way forward. If you don't have faith and dedication, there's no point even trying to go this way...
>
> —GMGD

VII. Takara no Chizu [宝の地図]

Perhaps the most valuable treasures contained in the *Ohba-Yūjin* notes are detailed charts of various disabling and destructive pressure points, along with a legend describing which of several possible body-weapons (finger/palm/fist/elbow/knee/foot) to employ when striking each.

Finger, palm, fist, and foot strikes are treated at length elsewhere in this work and others. What is often overlooked, however, is the power of the mid-joints—elbow and knee—not so much in terms of the manner of use, but rather with regard to the *timing* of that use. What Yūjin and other authorities stress is that these medial joints can be rapidly configured and deployed to *intercept* incoming strikes and *deter* follow-on attacks.

As a threshold matter, care must be taken to shape these joints appropriately. Both the knee and the elbow can be vulnerable targets depending on the way in which they are held, but they can also be forged into durable weapons by those who know the right method. For example, while <u>not</u> recommended, it is a fact that a baseball bat can be broken across the frontal aspect of a flexed knee (really, upper shin) with no resulting damage. Likewise, as illustrated by George Dillman on numerous occasions, the outer aspect of a flexed elbow (really, lower humerus bone) can smash through many inches or even feet of wood, brick, or ice.

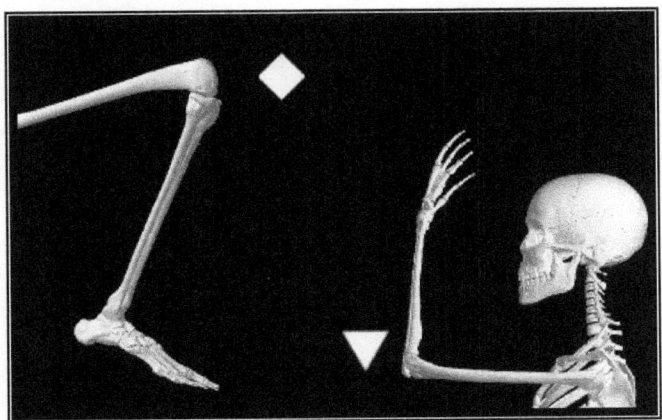

Now, couple this amazing structural strength with the fact that the knee can be elevated to intercept a leg strike much faster than a foot, and an elbow can be quickly flipped into the path of an incoming punch without appreciably deforming of the guard position of the hands, and you have a recipe for inflicting heavy damage on ballistic attacks from any quarter. Widely available videotape of Dillman's friend and training partner—Bruce Lee—counterstriking in this exact manner speaks volumes in this regard.

Ryūkyū Kempo

Turning to the targets themselves, then, the *Ohba* charts represent only one of many takes on this critical issue, from those contained in the *Bubishi*, to those illustrated in various acupuncture text books, to those presented to select instructors by Hohan Soken during his visit to the United States in 1972. What follows is an amalgam of all of these materials, refined in the crucible of a lifetime of study, and forged together in the fire of countless tactical engagements.

SPECIAL TACTICS—INTERCEPTION POINTS

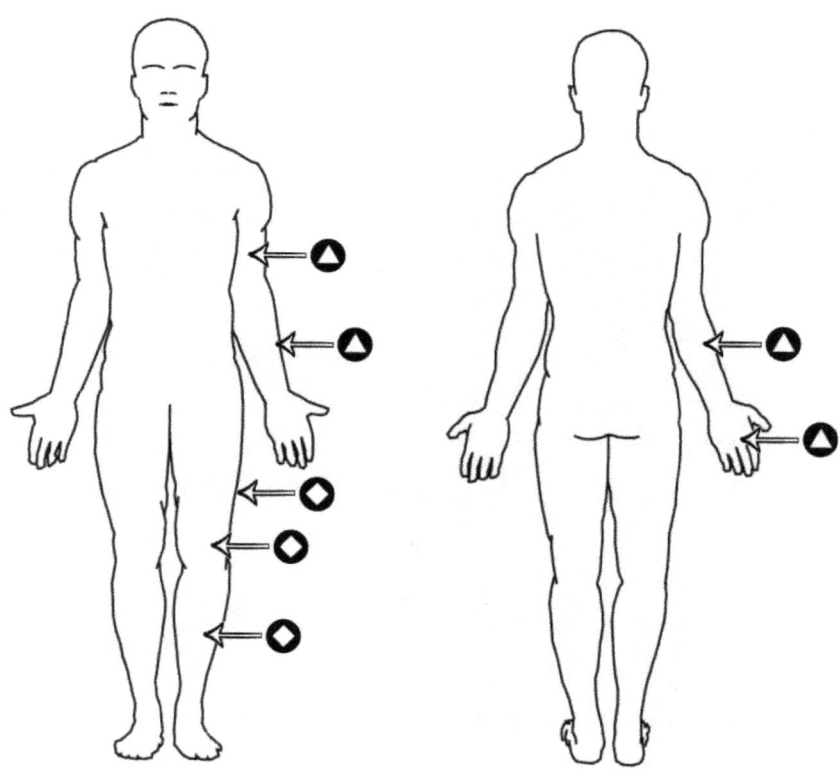

▲ Elbow interception points (from guard up/strike)

⬢ Knee interception points (from kick)

LETHAL POINTS

At the Deer Lake Camp, I had a machine that could trace the meridians and measure the strength of energy flow through them. It was calibrated to show a score of 100 at maximum (full energy at the beginning of life); most of the strong folks who trained there would read somewhere in the 80s. But if we hit the meridian, that number would drop instantly, and once it went below about 50 (half), they were gone!

I need you to be very careful with this next thing. There are many lethal points, but I am telling you now: **They are only to be used in life-or-death situations.**

For example, there is a meridian with one end deep inside your body. If you strike this point in the right way, with the right tool, the result can be lethal. The tool you want in the crane beak from *Gojushiho*. In fact, this entire technique is contained in the form—angle, direction, location…

—GMGD

Ryūkyū Kempo

VIII. Higashi to Nishi [東と西]

The yin/yang qualities of the meridians and the flow of the diurnal cycle of the organs is well established in Eastern medicine, and well understood in the art of pressure point fighting.

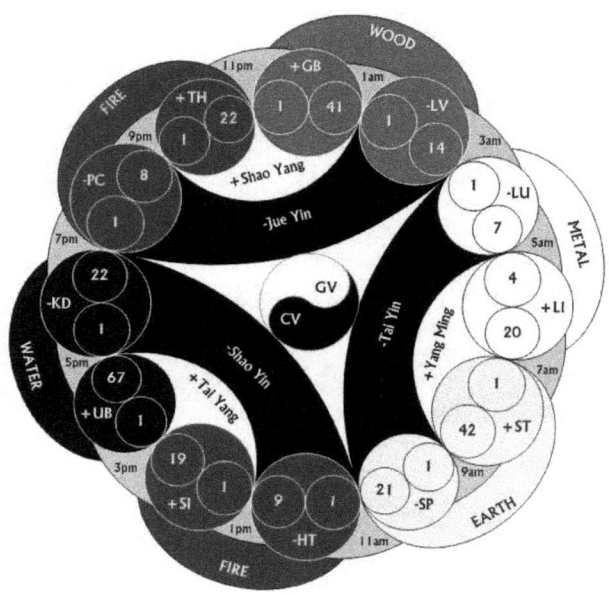

The *Ohba-Yūjin* notes, however, bring something new to the table where these Eastern concepts intersect with Western science.

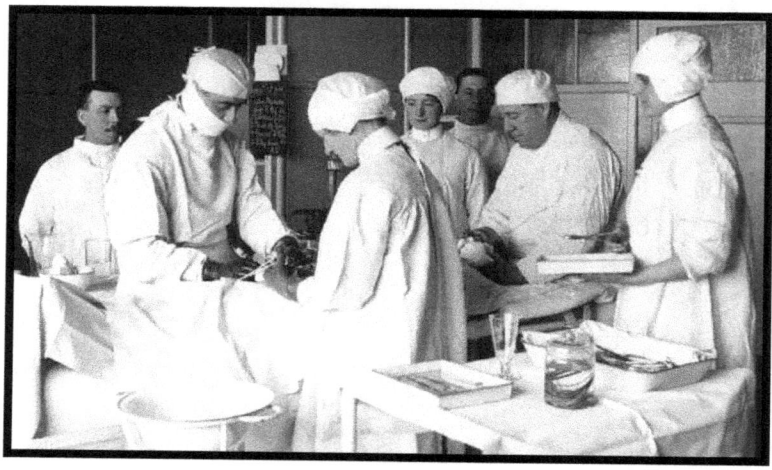

SPECIAL TARGETS—INTERSECTION POINTS

"Intersection points" occur where three vital characteristics converge:

- The location of meridian/partner meridian;
- The location of/access to the actual organ;
- Known instances illustrating the power of strikes to these targets.

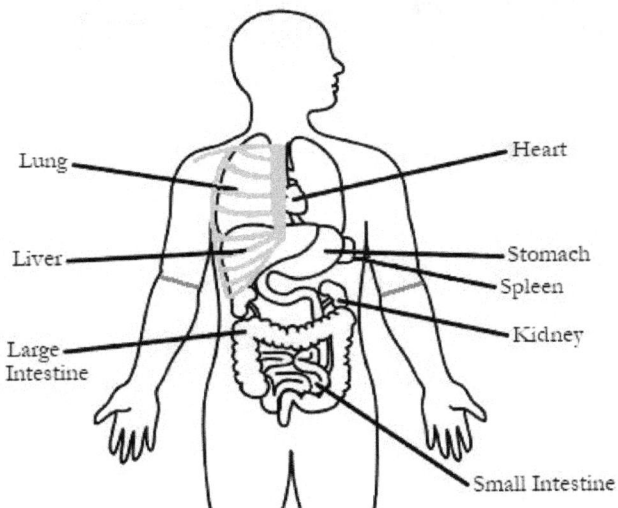

1. **"Village Rain" Point/Lung-1:** Located on the upper lateral chest, level with the first intercostal space, six *cun* from the thoracic midline, this point overlies the **actual organ**, and, as the Editor can attest from firsthand experience, with the right direction and energy, a strike to this target can cause immediate bodily dysfunction and total system shut-down.

2. **"Gentle Snow" Point/Liver-13:** Located on the lateral side of the abdomen, below the free end of the eleventh floating rib (from whence the **actual organ** can be accessed on the **right** side), Bernard Hopkins used this technique to knock out Oscar De La Hoya in a 2004 boxing match.

3. **"Moon Shadow" Point/Spleen-17:** Located on the lateral aspect of the chest in the fifth intercostal space, six *cun* from the anterior midline (from whence the **actual organ** can be accessed on the opponent's **left** side), MMA legend Bas Rutten has employed this strike to drop opponents so reliably that he has published several video training segments on the correct application of this technique.

Ryūkyū Kempo

4. **"Rear Lightning" Point/Bladder-51:** Located on the back, three *cun* lateral to the twelfth vertebra, this point lies over its **partner organs**, the kidneys. If struck correctly on either side—especially with a kick—it will reliably, *"block breathing and destroy stamina."* Roy Jones Jr. used this technique to defeat Virgil Hill in 1998, and George Foreman routinely employs it to finish off his opponents.

5. **"Root" Point/Pericardium:** This point is deemed to be too dangerous to present in a publicly accessible forum and will only be taught by qualified instructors, in person, to trusted students.

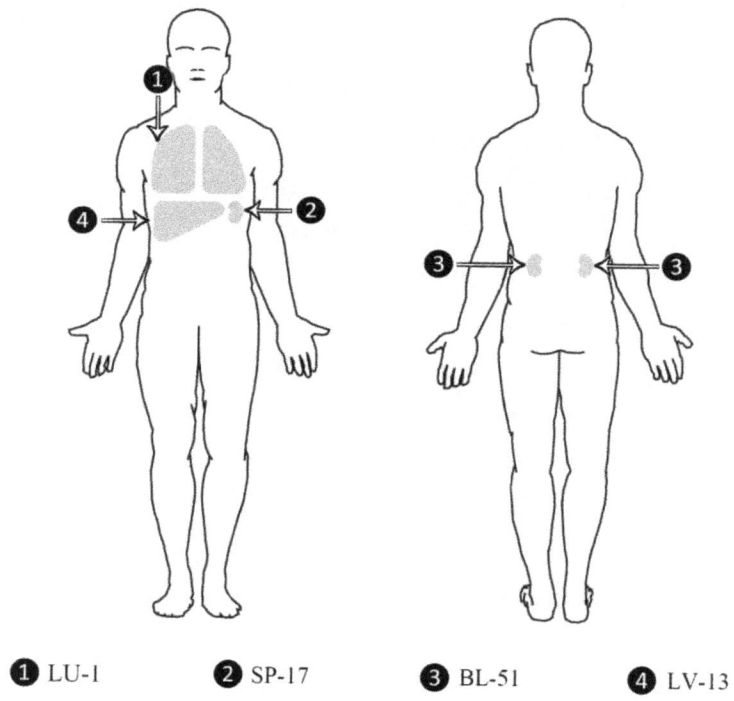

❶ LU-1   ❷ SP-17   ❸ BL-51   ❹ LV-13

INTERSECTION POINTS

There is *absolutely* a connection between the meridian and the actual organ. If you apply a pressure point on a particular meridian, and you aim it at the same actual organ, it makes the effect so much stronger. For example, with reverse wrist lock, if you torque the large intestine point in the direction of that same organ, you can drop your opponent like a rock!

—GMGD

IX. Iron Shirt Energy

Ohba also made arrangements for Dillman to visit the Hand Healing School in Gifu, where he got to work directly with two of the clinic's top healers: *Zatuo Noda* and *Hideaki Itoh*.

REIKI

After the demonstration at the jujitsu school, Ohba took me to the hand healing *(reiki)* school. I was able to talk meridian theory and point practice with the head of the school for hours. And I think between watching me teach his son, demonstrate at the jujitsu school, and work with the *reiki* teachers, Ohba finally decided that I would be able to make good use of the notes that had been in his family for so many years. As soon as he offered them to me, I signaled my wife to put them in her bag right away before he changed his mind! I've had that family study ever since then, but it's only recently that we have finished translating them all.
—GMGD

BODY ARMOR

The human body can be strengthened like armor. If you use the proper external and internal exercises together, you can harden the muscles and make them as tough as iron! And you can also orient your body to make it stronger: For example, if you twist the palm out at an angle in the turning point in *Seisan*, it makes the arm much stronger and better able to resist forward pressure (I got this particular piece of the puzzle from an Indian Chief on a North American reservation).
—GMGD

Ryūkyū Kempo

X. Control

If the "intersection points" may be said to cause total system failure when applied correctly, at the other end of the medico-legal spectrum are the "control points"—those places where the exertion of a moderate amount of force can induce compliance without risking serious injury (making them ideal tools for law enforcement professionals).

SPECIAL TARGETS II—CONTROL POINTS

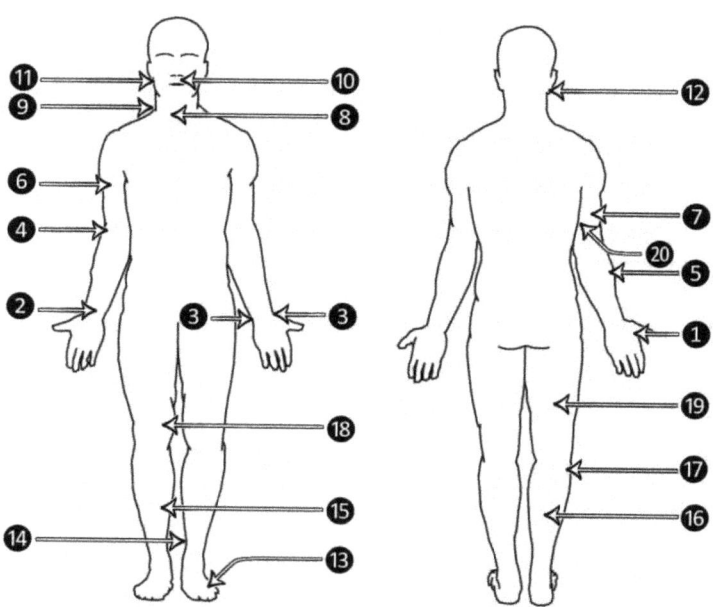

❶ LI-4: Opens fist
❷ P-6: Closes/weakens fist
❸ LU-8 & HT-6: Bends wrist
❹ LU-5: Bends elbow (inside)
❺ LI-10: Bends elbow (outside)
❻ P-2: Releases shoulder (front)
❼ TW-12: Releases shoulder (back)
❽ LI-17: Controls torso (out)
❾ LI-18: Controls torso (in)
❿ GV-26: Controls head (back)
⓫ ST-6: Contols head (side)
⓬ TW-17: Controls head (up/forward)
⓭ GB-42: Pins foot
⓮ SP-6: Controls calf (out)
⓯ ST-37: Controls calf (back)
⓰ BL-57: Controls calf (forward)
⓱ BL-40: Released knee (forward)
⓲ SP-10: Releases knee (out)
⓳ BL-37: Controls thigh (forward)
⓴ SP-21: Controls torso (in)

As martial artists walk the path of their ancestors, and progress from novice to disciple to veteran, their knowledge will certainly increase, but so too should their wisdom. While the young brown belt probably *can* defeat all comers, the mature black belt must consider whether he *should*. And it is most appropriate in a realm where experience translates directly into effectiveness that the more powerful a master becomes, the more restraint he shows. This is truly the case with George Dillman, who has always been an advocate of the *humane* use pressure points and the healing effects of the arts, but particularly so in his latter years.

BETTER WITH AGE

I actually had to knock someone out when I was aged 75! These techniques work no matter how old you get. And especially if you set it up right, Stomach-5 is one of the most reliable "off-switches" for the human body, regardless of type. But there's often a better way. If you apply even slight pressure to a particular point on the nerve in the neck, it weakens the opponent's entire body. You can test this by simply placing your thumb on this point and asking your partner to try and pick you up (they won't be able to).

—GMGD

XI. *TSUKI NO SHŪKI* [月の周期]

From this same ancient source comes a reference to an often-neglected cycle impacting the flow of energy: *Tsuki no shūki*—the lunar phases. Before taking a leap of faith into the esoteric, however, let's ground ourselves firmly in the concrete:

- **Planetary Rotation:** There can be no doubt that the turning of the earth has numerous practical effects on tactical decision-making. To take a simple example which has endured, from the age of the *samurai* to present day military operations, the position of the sun in the sky is an important consideration when it comes to both vision and visibility.

- **Planetary Orbit:** Likewise, the progression of the earth around the sun—which causes the seasons—is an important consideration in many ways. Experienced knife-fighters will tell you, for instance, that clothing choices occasioned by the ambient temperature have a significant effect on the way they work their art.

- **Lunar Orbit:** Doesn't it stand to reason, then, that the third major circular trajectory in our skies—that of the an object about a quarter the size of our planet, orbiting us at 2300 miles an hour, only thirty times our diameter away—should also have a substantial impact on life on earth? Well it does. Even leaving aside such massive and well-known phenomena as the rise and fall of the tides, the position of the moon relative to the earth at any given time also has reliable, measurable effects on marine life, birds, and insects, primarily through its interaction with the planetary magnetic field. Given our familiarity with the diurnal cycle, it should come as no surprise to learn that when one of the ancient masters wrote the verse on the following page, he was likely referring to the (on average) twelve complete lunar cycles during the indicated timeframe.

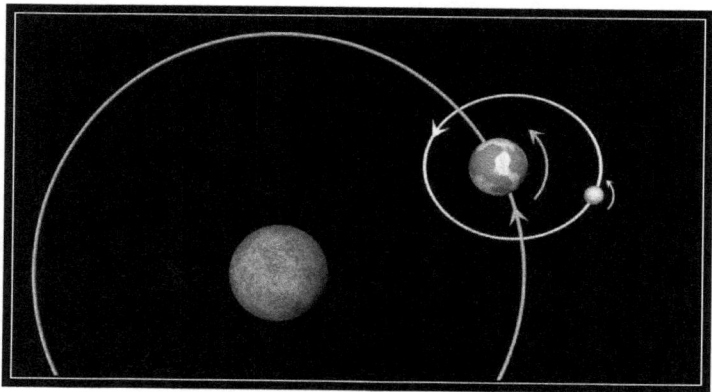

> *"To learn the essence of the target areas that control life and death, you must know the following: the Four Seasons of Spring, Summer, Autumn, and Winter are divided into the <u>twelve</u> time periods to judge life and death."*

IT'S ALL CONNECTED

Of course the phase of the moon matters! So do the seasons. So does the direction you are facing. You need to understand that it's *all* connected. West is metal (relative to East). East is wood (relative to West). Remember it this way: Where was the gold rush? And where is Penn's wood? Good, now back to the lunar phases. I once taught a seminar in New Zealand (twice actually) where we went all down the length of the island during the period leading up to the full moon. I told my host: *"Just watch: I'm going to do the same (fire) technique on people, the same way, every place we stop, but you'll see the effect increase as the moon phase changes."* And it did—it worked like a charm!

—GMGD

The tried-and-true lesson here, then, is that it may be helpful to employ certain kinds of techniques in response to the corresponding energetic conditions at a given time and place. At its simplest, this means taking into account lighting, temperature, and the like in tactical planning. At its most sublime, it means attuning yourself to the heartbeat of the universe.

- **Fire Techniques:** While certain techniques are considered fire *per se* (e.g. front stance), as discussed earlier, almost any technique can be performed with fire energy. Fire energy is aggressive, rapid, and relentless, but not heavy. Directions traditionally associated with this element are upward and inward. A flurry of jabs, for example, has fire energy.

- **Water Techniques:** Water energy is receptive, steady, and patient. Directions traditionally associated with this element are downward and outward. A redirecting parry, for example, is the epitome of water energy.

- **Wood Techniques:** Wood energy is rooted, durable, and flexible. The direction traditionally associated with this element is outward (expanding). Joint locks are good examples of wood energy at work.

- **Metal Techniques:** Metal energy is hard and precise. The direction traditionally associated with this element is forward, as employed in a direct, committed thrust or strike to a particularly vulnerable point.

- **Earth Techniques:** Earth energy is heavy and powerful. Directions traditionally associated with this element are inward and down. Throws employing the practitioner's and/or the opponent's body weight are archetypal earth techniques.

XII. The Charts: Special Meridians and Points

Most practitioners are familiar with the twelve standard meridians and the three hundred and sixty odd points which populate them. Many are also familiar with the extraordinary meridians and their associated points. But only a select few truly understand and appreciate the significance and interplay of specialized combinations involving set-up points, junction points, horary points, and the like:

- **Extraordinary Meridians:**
  Conception Vessel (Ren Mai) [任脈]: Perineum to chin;
  Governing Vessel (Du Mai) [督脈]: Coccyx to upper lip;
  Girdle Vessel (Dai Mai) [帶脈]: Below navel, around midsection;*
  Penetrating Vessel (Chong Mai) [衝脈]: Abdomen/perineum to lip;*
  Yin linking vessel (Yin Wei Mai) [陰維脈]: Shin to trachea;*
  Yang linking vessel (Yang Wei Mai) [陽維脈]: Heel to back of head;*
  Yin Heel Vessel (Yin Qiao Mai) [陰蹻脈]: Outside foot to inside eye;*
  Yang Heel Vessel (Yang Qiao Mai) [陽蹻脈]: Heel to back of head.*

> * These channels differ from the standard in that they 'borrow' points from other meridians and their course often runs deep within the body.

- **Source Points:** There is one *"yuan* point" for each standard meridian. Located near the hands and feet, these are the places where the *chi/qi* first gathers, and from which it is distributed to the meridians.

Lung	LU-9
Large Intestine	LI-4
Stomach	ST-42
Spleen	SP-3
Heart	HT-7
Small Intestine	SI-4
Bladder	BL-64
Kidney	KI-3
Pericardium	PC-7
Triple Warmer	TW-4
Gall Bladder	GB-40
Liver	LV-3

- **Accumulating Points:** In balanced counterpoint to the source points, "*xi* points" are like shallow points in the 'river' where *chi/qi* slows and collects, and are therefore often used to clear their respective channels.

Lung	LU-6
Large Intestine	LI-7
Stomach	ST-34
Spleen	SP-8
Heart	HT-6
Small Intestine	SI-6
Bladder	BL-63, BL-59
Kidney	KI-5, KI-8, KI-9
Pericardium	PC-4
Triple Warmer	TW-7
Gall Bladder	GB-36, GB-35
Liver	LV-6

- **Alarm Points:** There is one "*mu* point" for each standard meridian. Located on the chest, they are used both to detect and treat maladies involving the associated meridian.

Lung	LU-1
Large Intestine	ST-25
Stomach	CV-12
Spleen	LV-13
Heart	CV-14
Small Intestine	CV-4
Bladder	CV-3
Kidney	GB-25
Pericardium	CV-17
Triple Warmer	CV-5
Gall Bladder	GB-24
Liver	LV-14

- **Associated Points:** The twelve "*shu* points," located on the back along the Bladder Meridian, correspond to a particular organ or body part and have the same diagnostic relationship with those parts as the Alarm Points.

Lung	BL-13
Large Intestine	BL-25
Stomach	BL-21
Spleen	BL-20
Heart	BL-15
Small Intestine	BL-27
Bladder	BL-28
Kidney	BL-23
Pericardium	BL-14
Triple Warmer	BL-22
Gall Bladder	BL-19
Liver	BL-18

- **Horary Points:** There is one horary point for each standard meridian. Located near the hands and feet, these are points that correspond to the *same* element in the creative cycle, and are most powerful during that meridian's period of ascendancy in the diurnal cycle.

Lung	LU-8
Large Intestine	LI-1
Stomach	ST-36
Spleen	SP-3
Heart	HT-8
Small Intestine	SI-5
Bladder	BL-66
Kidney	KI-10
Pericardium	PC-8
Triple Warmer	TW-6
Gall Bladder	GB-41
Liver	LV-1

Ryūkyū Kempō

- **Junction Points:** There is one *"luo* point" for each standard meridian. Located near the hands and feet, these are points that link one meridian to its partner meridian, and can be used to regulate the balance of energy between these symbiotic channels.

Lung	LI-6
Large Intestine	LU-7
Stomach	SP-4
Spleen	ST-40
Heart	SI-7
Small Intestine	HT-5
Bladder	KI-4
Kidney	BL-58
Pericardium	TW-5
Triple Warmer	PC-6
Gall Bladder	LV-5
Liver	GB-37

- **Command Points:** Also known as "element points," these lie along the standard meridians between the fingers and elbows/toes and knees, and contain "dynamic" energy, giving them powerful clinical utility. Each set of points represents all five elements.

Meridian	Wood	Fire	Earth	Metal	Water
Lung	LU-11	LU-10	LU-9	LU-8	LU-5
Large Intestine	LI-1	LI-2	LI-3	LI-5	LI-11
Stomach	ST-45	ST-44	ST-43	ST-41	ST-36
Spleen	SP-1	SP-2	SP-3	SP-5	SP-9
Heart	HT-9	HT-8	HT-7	HT-4	HT-3
Small Intestine	SI-1	SI-2	SI-3	SI-5	SI-8
Bladder	BL-67	BL-66	BL-65	BL-60	BL-40
Kidney	KI-1	KI-2	KI-3	KI-7	KI-10
Pericardium	PC-9	PC-8	PC-7	PC-5	PC-3
Triple Warmer	TW-1	TW-2	TW-3	TW-6	TW-10
Gall Bladder	GB-44	GB-43	GB-41	GB-38	GB-34
Liver	LV-1	LV-2	LV-3	LV-4	LV-8

- **Tonifying Points:** There is one "*bu* point" for each standard meridian. Located near the hands and feet, these are points that correspond to the *previous* element in the creative cycle (the 'mother'), and are used to strengthen the energy in the meridian on which they are located.

Lung	LU-9
Large Intestine	LI-11
Stomach	ST-41
Spleen	SP-2
Heart	HT-9
Small Intestine	SI-3
Bladder	BL-67
Kidney	KI-7
Pericardium	PC-9
Triple Warmer	TW-3
Gall Bladder	GB-43
Liver	LV-8

- **Sedation Points:** There is one "*xie* point" for each standard meridian. Located near the hands and feet, these are points that correspond to the *subsequent* element in the creative cycle (the 'child'), and are used to reduce energy in the meridian on which they are located.

Lung	LU-5
Large Intestine	LI-2
Stomach	ST-45
Spleen	SP-5
Heart	HT-7
Small Intestine	SI-8
Bladder	BL-65
Kidney	KI-1
Pericardium	PC-7
Triple Warmer	TW-10
Gall Bladder	GB-38
Liver	LV-2

Ryūkyū Kempo

- **Miracle Points:** The twelve *"tsing* points" are located on the tips of the toes and fingers, and are commonly used to treat ailments when a more specific treatment protocol cannot be determined.

Lung	LU-11
Large Intestine	LI-1
Stomach	ST-45
Spleen	SP-1
Heart	HT-9
Small Intestine	SI-1
Bladder	BL-67
Kidney	KI-1
Pericardium	PC-9
Triple Warmer	TW-1
Gall Bladder	GB-44
Liver	LV-1

- **Set-up Points:** Of perhaps greatest import to pressure point fighters, however, are the "set up points," the activation of which dramatically amplifies the effect of stimulating a corresponding point *after* the fact.

Lung	LU-5 (inside intercept)	LU-1
Lung	LI-10 (outside intercept)	LU-1
Large Intestine	PC-6, LI-10	LI-17/18
Stomach	LU-8, PC-6, HT-6 (wrist manacle)	ST-9
Spleen	SP-6 (opposite side better)	SP-11
Spleen	LU-8, PC-6, HT-6 (wrist manacle)	SP-17
Heart	SI-8	HT-1
Heart	TW-8/TW-9	HT-2
Small Intestine	LU-8, LU-5	SI-15
Bladder	LU-5	BL-51
Kidney	SI-18	KI-21
Pericardium	LU-8, PC-6, HT-6 (wrist manacle)	PC-1
Triple Warmer	TW-6, TW-7, TW-8 (TW ditch)	TW-11/TW-12
Gall Bladder	LI-10	GB 13-15
Gall Bladder	TW-11/TW-12	GB-20
Liver	TW-11/TW-12	LV-13

SET-UP POINTS: CHART I

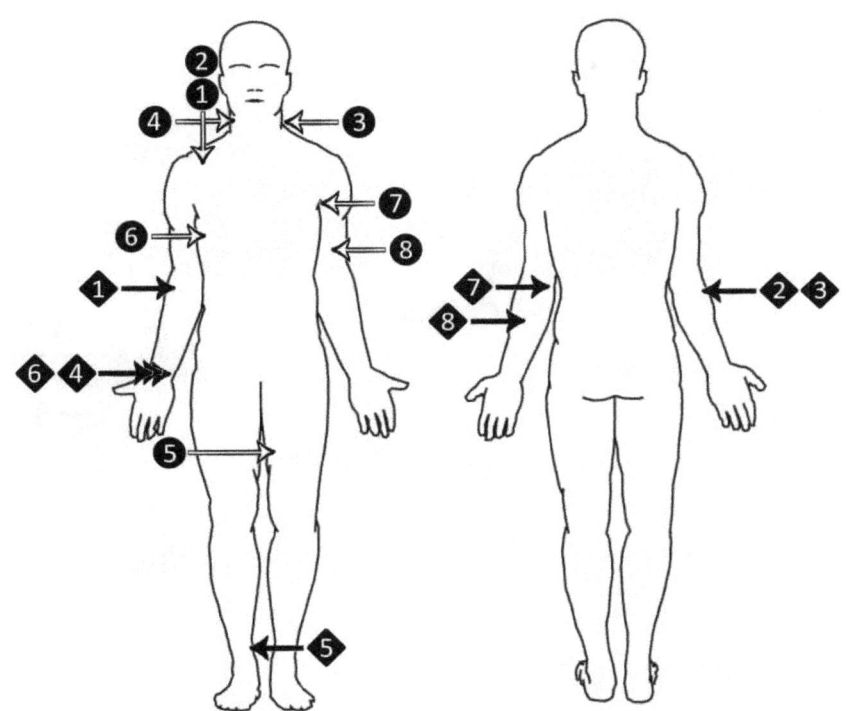

- ◆1 LU-5 ●1 LU-1
- ◆2 LI-10 ●2 LU-1
- ◆3 LI-10 ●3 LI-17
- ◆4 LU-8/PE-6/HT-6 ●4 ST-9
- ◆5 SP-6 ●5 SP-11
- ◆6 LU-8/PE-6/HT-6 ●6 SP-17
- ◆7 SI-8 ●7 HT-1
- ◆8 TW-8/TW-9 ●8 HT-2

Ryūkyū Kempo

SET-UP POINTS: CHART II

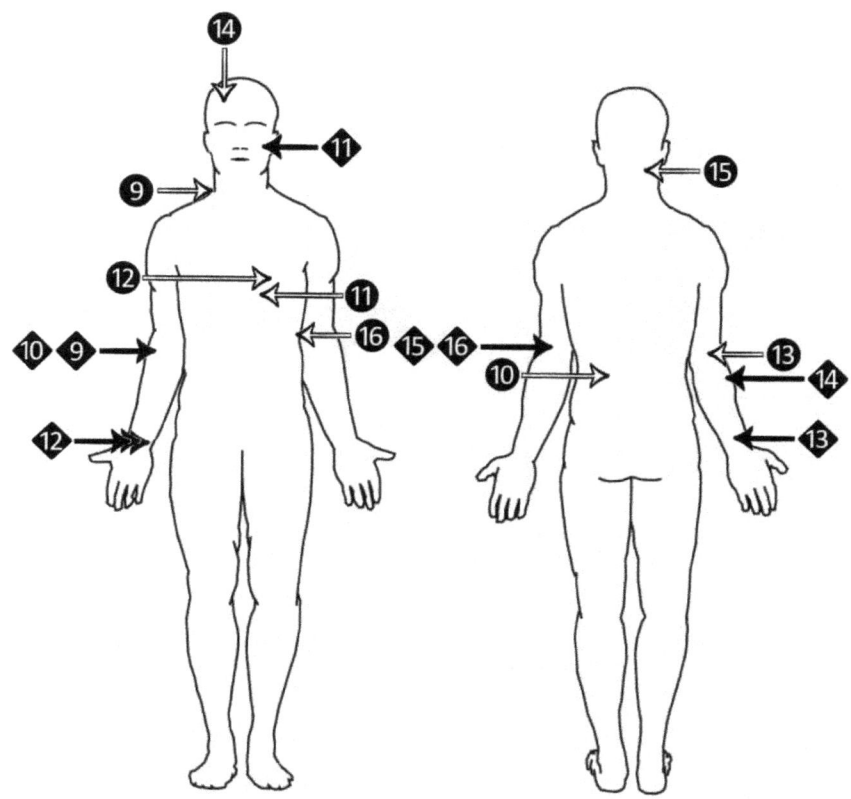

- ◆9 LU-5   ●9 SI-15
- ◆10 LU-5 ●10 BL-51
- ◆11 SI-18 ●11 KI-21
- ◆12 LU-8/PC-6/HT-6   ●12 PC-1
- ◆13 TW-6/TW-7/TW-8   ●13 TW-11/TW-12
- ◆14 LI-10   ●14 GB-13/GB-14/GB-15
- ◆15 TW-11/TW-12   ●15 GB-20
- ◆16 TW-11/TW-12   ●16 LV-13

- **Organic Overload Points:** A sub-category of the set-up points are the organic overload points. Energetically speaking, there are two main approaches to disabling an attacker: Choking off the energy supply ("black tiger") and overloading it ("white crane"). Overloading is in many ways easier to achieve, and is accomplished by striking one or more meridians (injecting energy) in the correct manner and order.

Accessible Meridian: It is undeniable that many—if not most—attacks are initiated by the arms, and are also commonly defended using the arms. Given the physical orientation of these offensive and defensive weapons, the most accessible channels for striking tend to be the inside and outside of the upper aspect of the forearm; the Lung and Large Intestine meridians respectively.

Achievable Points: In a perfect world, the practitioner would be able pick out the preferred point for striking, but in the cut-and-thrust of real world engagements, he may have to settle for any of a number of possibilities along the chosen channel (LU-8, LU-6, **LU-5**, LU-4, LU-3/LI-6, LI-7, LI-8, **LI-10**, LI-14).

Organic Sequence: Rather than contenting himself with merely invoking the elemental cycle, following the Chinese cosmological progression known as, "1-2-5-8-12," the master practitioner may choose to follow the organic cycle (... Liver—Lung—Large Intestine—Stomach—Spleen...) in order to achieve a more precise effect. Using this model, striking a point on the Lung meridian—particularly *in the same direction* as the flow of that channel—will amplify the flow of energy in the Large Intestine (child) meridian. In turn, striking the Large Intestine meridian in the right manner will have a similar effect on the Stomach channel, and so on...

The Points: It is interesting to note that the arm-intercepting strikes described above position the opponent perfectly to access the follow-up points. For example, a hard strike to the outer aspect of the forearm (along the Large Intestine meridian) will both prime and produce access to appropriate targets on the Stomach meridian (such as ST-5 and ST-9). Similarly, a firm blow to the inner aspect of the attacking arm (along the Lung meridian) will deliver appropriate follow-up points (like LI-17 and LI-18). Whether this phenomenon is the result of arcane energy flow or simple bio-mechanics is largely irrelevant; what truly matters is that it *works*.

Set up: LU-8, LU-6, **LU-5**, LU-4, LU-3	Follow-on: ST-5, ST-9
Set-up: LI-6, LI-7, LI-8, **LI-10**, LI-14	Follow-on: LI-17, LI-18

Ryūkyū Kempō

The White Crane and the Black Tiger: Systemic overloads—short circuits if you will—are relatively easy to explain and achieve through striking, and are sometimes referred to as "white crane" techniques because of the flash of light that many experience when they are applied. System drainage (power cuts, frequently described as "black tiger" techniques) are more complex. Sometimes used in TCM to treat energy excesses, the idea behind the *draining* approach is to block or even reverse the flow of energy in a given meridian, causing it to diminish significantly or even back up into the previous (parent) channel in the organic cycle. Energy drainage is often easier to achieve through seizing or choking than it is through striking.

XIII. Special Tools: Tetsuwa/Kannawa [鉄輪/鐶縄]

Another lesser known training method discussed in the *Ohba-Yūjin* notes is that of ring *("tetsuwa"/"kannawa")* practice. With its roots in ancient Chinese conditioning systems, ring training—iron and otherwise—takes many forms, including practical applications when employed in conjunction with a rope in the art of *hojojutsu*.

♦ **Single Small Iron Ring:** In keeping with the "low weight/high repetitions" theory of conditioning, adding even a modest load to a variety of hand and leg techniques—as *Sifu* Leo Fong regularly does—can improve their unencumbered performance immeasurably.

♦ **Multiple Small Iron Rings:** In much the same way that adopting the horse stance for long periods of time alone can work well to strengthen the lower body, simply holding a number of heavy iron rings on the arms can do wonders for conditioning upper body musculature.

♦ **Single Large Wooden Ring:** In addition to the heavy metal versions, wooden rings are often used in a variety of arts—especially in solo practice—to train for proper hand position; to perfect tandem movements; and to improve sensitivity.

♦ **Single Small Wooden Ring:** A more compact version of this training tool is favored when working to refine accuracy, speed, and timing. There is also a flexible model available for improving and testing grip strength (like breaking a board to ensure minimum strike force, if you can't crush a five inch wooden ring, your touch/rub strength needs work…)

XIV. The Eyes Have It

According to the National Institute of Health (NIH), about one in fifteen Americans has been treated using acupuncture. In Japanese and Chinese communities, that ratio is closer to one in four.

It is difficult—if not impossible—to engage in the deep study of the Eastern martial arts without an understanding of certain aspects of Eastern thought, among them, Five Element theory and the flow of *chi* or *ki* in the body. As a result, acupuncture skeptics tend to be fewer and further between in this realm than in the general population,

Nevertheless, die-hard skeptics who are compelled to accept the *existence* of acupuncture pressure points will sometimes shift the focus of their complaints to claiming that these points are too difficult to employ in real combat. To this, George Dillman says: *"Just watch me..."*

> **REFLECTIONS ON THE PATH**
>
> The more I think back, the more I realize that I was *always* on this path. From my time with Harry Smith in the early Sixties, when he showed us *Tatsuo Shimabuku's* teachings (striking ST-5 and ST-6 simultaneously; the GB-20 killing technique from *Suansu*, etc...); to Bruce Lee pointing me toward the *Black Belt Magazine* article on 'electrical' points; to Danny Pai's *"If a man can't stand/see/breath"* techniques; to tournaments at Jhoon Rhee's school; to my time with *Hohan Soken* and *Seiyu Oyata*—it seems like the Universe was charting this course for me...
>
> —GMGD

Let's talk rough numbers for a minute: According to the World Health Organization (WHO), there are 361 "classical" acupuncture points on the human body. According to Dillman, the size of the *clinical* area of activation is about the same as the human pupil (about a tenth of an inch), whereas the size of the *combat* area of activation is about the same as the entire eyeball (not just the iris—about an inch—roughly the same as a quarter).

Diameter   24.26 mm (0.955 in)

Note: Reference to the human eye as a means of illustrating the relative sizes of the different areas of activation should <u>not</u> be misinterpreted as indicating that this is an appropriate location for needling—it is not!

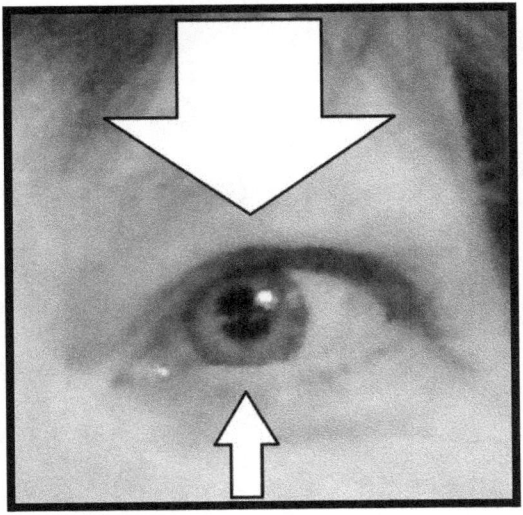

One 'round inch' has an area of about 8/10 of a 'square inch,' meaning that the combined areas of activation of the 361 classical points add up to about 280 square inches. The average human is covered by about 2,800 square inches of skin. Accordingly, combat pressure point activation areas account for about one tenth of the total surface of the human body.

Now, picture a (non-regulation) dartboard with ten segments (instead of the usual twenty).

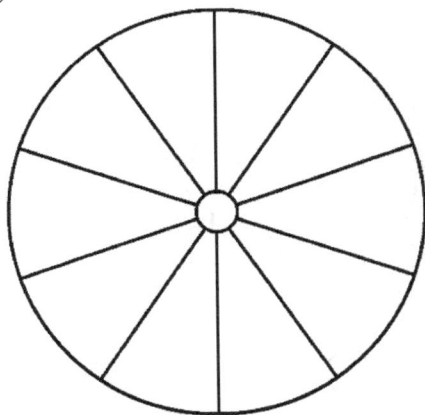

Ryūkyū Kempo

Using this as an analog for the surface area of the human body, the bullseye represents the *clinical* area of activation, but the rest of the board illustrates the *combat* area of activation, shown more-or-less to scale in these images.

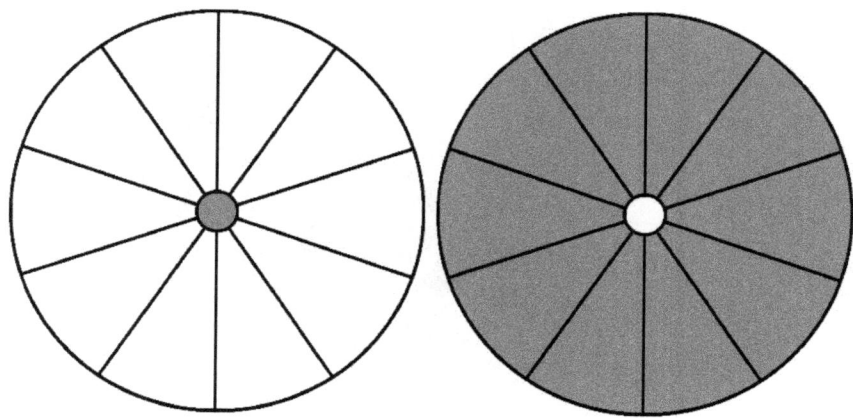

Since roughly one tenth of the skin's surface area is within the combat area of activation, simply throwing a 'dart' at random toward this target gives rise to a one-in-ten chance of hitting a pressure point.

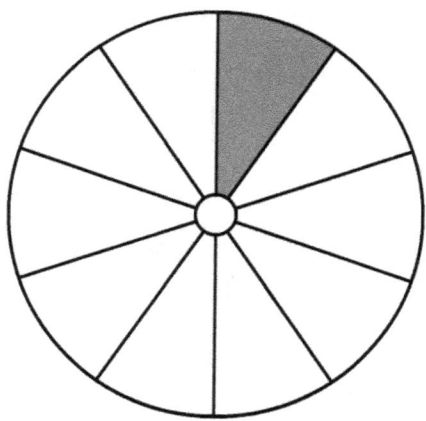

But there is more. The arms and head—two of the most available and effective target areas—are more densely packed with points than the rest of the body. The head/neck region contains about 58 points, and the arms, about 47. Given that each of these regions represents about 9% of the body's total surface area (according to Western medicine's Wallace Rule), the ratio of active to inactive areas is more like 1:5 in these target-rich environments.

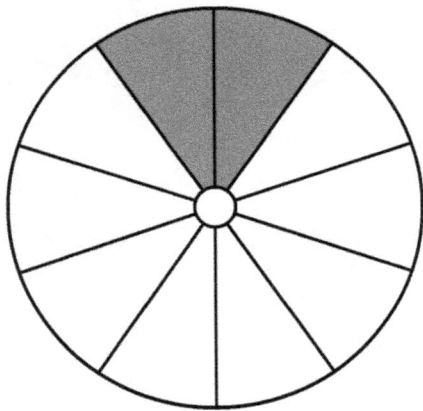

Moreover, we strike using fists, not darts. The surface area of the typical fist is more than one square inch. For the typical fighter, it's more like six. Thus, each strike represents six chances of hitting an area of activation.

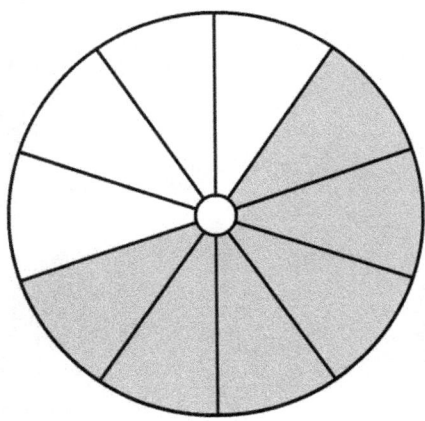

When you put all of this together, the odds of being able to hit an area of activation, even randomly, increase to a very high degree of probability—certainly enough to warrant their use, especially when layered in with techniques which operate on collateral principles, like disrupting balance or organic function.

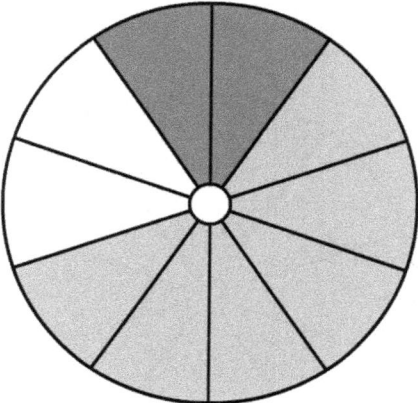

In this regard, Dillman has more to say. His late teacher, Danny Pai, used to advocate ending a fight by taking away any of these three of the opponent's vital functions: The ability to see, the ability to breath, and the ability to stand. In this respect, the eye represents not just an analog, but also an actual target. No matter how much the opponent trains, he (or she) cannot armor the eye. And while eye strikes are extremely dangerous, and only to be used under dire circumstances, a slight flick of the fingers toward the ocular orbits will be sufficient in terms of speed, range, and power, to deter almost any attacker.

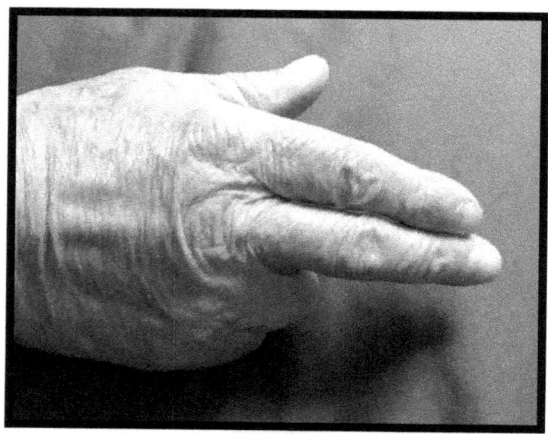

XV. Miscellany

> ◆ **The Power of Diamonds:** There is a reason that the diamond (◆) is used to introduce key points in this text: In the study of Ryūkyū Kempo, there seem to be an endless number of ways in which the power of "the diagonal" unlocks the secrets of this art; the three-quarter punch, the oblique strike, and the slanting block, to name just a few. For those who wish to take their practice to the next level, there is much to be absorbed from the study of this simple shape…

> ◆ **The Power of Sound:** While the topic of the power of sound is more fully treated in Chapter XIII of this work, it is well worth noting that the *Ohba-Yūjin* study corroborates the value of this practice, directing students to inject spirit into their technique by using the sounds: *"Ah!"* and *"Ya!"* (both 'up' sounds).

> ◆ **The Power of the Sword:** They say that to find someone's true passion, watch what they choose to do when the bills have been paid. In many ways, retirement is the ultimate expression of that paradigm, and in his superannuation, George Dillman finds himself increasingly drawn to the *katana*—particularly a centuries-old hand-forged blade in his collection. Having studied this weapon with Danny Pai, and taught its esoteric form, for many years, he says that in quieter moments, the ancient blade 'speaks' to him, illustrating hitherto unknown parallels with his beloved open-handed art.

Ryūkyū Kempō

XVI. THE FINAL LESSON: *RYU*—THE ETERNAL RIVER

In the early and intermediate stages, teaching martial arts is a little like sharing the 'fish' you have caught with hungry students. But in order to ascend to higher levels, the students must learn to 'fish' for themselves. This is in many ways the final lesson.

The ultimate method for preserving the ***ryu*** is not merely the flow of knowledge from *master* to *student;* it is also the evolution of *student* to *master.* Or, to turn the wheel full circle and end up where we began, in the insightful words of Grandmaster Chris Thomas: *"Because George Dillman can do it, I can do it too..."*

The ***ryu*** may be eternal, but man is not. George Dillman clearly had this ultimate truth in mind when providing the final word for this chapter:

> *As long as you remember my teachings, I will go on forever...*
>
> —GMGD

Based on these recent revelations, as you go about your daily routine, you can rest assured that the adventure continues; that the martial arts are truly the journey of a lifetime; and that a light still burns brightly in the castle of the man who has done more for this particular field of study than anyone in generations...

CHAPTER TWENTY-SEVEN:
The Next Generation

It is said that promotion to a teaching rank in the martial arts brings with it not just honor, but also a burden. As a teacher, the martial artist is required to carry on the tradition, to help preserve the system, and to pay respect to those who have gone before. One way to do this is to bring new people to the arts.

Ryūkyū Kempo

And not just with an eye to making sure that the student body remains robust, but also with the long-term goal of creating new masters in their own right. If the student's ability one day exceeds the teacher's, this should be cause for rejoicing, not recriminating. Because this is the best way any teacher can repay his debt to the past masters.

George Dillman honors this principle in many ways. He has brought a vast number of new faces to the martial table, and has also opened the eyes of many who were already there to begin with. He has trained some students from the ground up, and adopted others who may have lost their way along the path. And he is one of the few headmasters who not only tolerates, but encourages his senior people to take on much of the responsibility for teaching, even when he is present.

From this, it is clear that he recognizes that the future of his art—his legacy—lies with his students. With that in mind, the voices of the next generation of Ryūkyū Kempo masters form an indispensable part of the story.

◆ PAUL BOWMAN, UK ◆

I remember the first time I met Professor Dillman. I attended a seminar where he took me to one side and said, "Look around Paul, look at the size of all these people. In a real fight do you think you could beat these guys?" He continued, "You're a good martial artist and a good blocker but you need the pressure points at your size." I am 5'3" and he was so right. That was over twenty years ago. The first person I knocked out was 6'6"! So I say: "Thank you, you have made my martial arts work, my mentor, my friend and true gentleman, Professor George Dillman."

◆ GARY BRINCAT, MICHIGAN, USA ◆

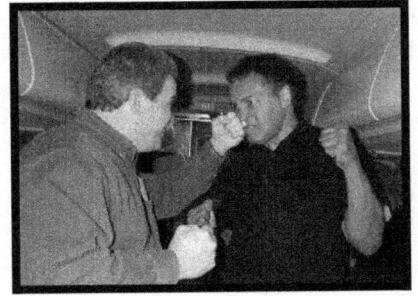

My first exposure to Master Dillman was at a seminar in Indiana. Maybe because I sat up front, or maybe because I appeared interested, or maybe because I did not have a Dillman patch on my gi yet, I was chosen by Master Dillman to be his uke. Master Dillman was teaching finger locks and control techniques and proceeded to use the finger lock to put me up on my tiptoes. I was fully extended on my toes as high as I could; he had me at the point that I felt if I relaxed even a millimeter, my fingers would break.

He then started a three minute lecture, with me on my tiptoes, straining to save my hand. He would turn me to the right, then back to the left as he spoke on a couple of topics, none of which I remember. All I remember was how relieved I was when he released the finger lock. He knew I was on the edge, and where the edge was, and just held me there while orating.

◆ ◆ ◆ ◆ ◆

In May of 2009 I was on my way to the Camp to train with Master Dillman and was pulled over twenty miles from the camp by a Pennsylvania state trooper. He asked me where I was going in such a hurry. I told him I was on my way to train with Master Dillman at the Muhammad Ali Camp. The trooper handed me back my license and registration with a warning to slow down and told me to have a nice day.

◆ ◆ ◆ ◆ ◆

On another occasion I was in the Detroit Airport waiting for a flight to California with my family. As I waited, I was reading Master Dillman's book: Kyusho-Jitsu: The Dillman Method of Pressure Point Fighting. In the book is a picture of Muhammad Ali and Master Dillman from when they trained together. As I read, my wife nudged me and said, "Look who just walked in." I looked up to see Muhammad Ali and his family; they were on the same flight to California. I took the book over to the Champ and asked him to sign his picture. He was shocked to see I had a picture of him at the airport. His wife asked me, "What book is that," and when I told her it was a George Dillman book, she smiled and said, "Yes we know George." Ali gladly signed the book, and after we were in the air, he left first class to come see me in coach.

◆ DEXTER BROWN, NEW YORK, USA ◆

I first met George Dillman in 1989 in Pottsville, Pennsylvania. Being a New York City narcotics officer and holding three black belts in different styles, I was looking for anything that would help me to apprehend drug suspects faster and with minimal injury to me as well as them. So after reading about Mr. Dillman's techniques in *Black Belt* magazine and seeing them on his first set of videos, I decided to attend a seminar and see if the Dillman method was for real!

At the seminar Mr. Dillman started teaching the now-famous arm points (2-4-6). Being a relatively big guy (6'2" and 225 lbs.) to my surprise, Grandmaster Dillman went right after me. He started cranking on my arm and the next thing I knew I was on the seat of my pants wondering what happened! This happened two or three more times, leaving me feeling that this was something I had to learn. The rest is history. We started a student-teacher relationship which was more like buddy-buddy. Not only did he personally teach me his method of pressure points fighting, but we became the best of friends.

I began to use my new found skills on the mean streets of New York, reporting back to Grandmaster Dillman frequently. With his help and mentoring, I was able to perfect techniques that even worked wonders on people under the influence of drugs like PCP. These techniques revolutionized my martial art skills, and are presently being taught and used by law enforcement agencies throughout the United States and overseas.

◆ MATT BROWN, NEW HAMPSHIRE, USA ◆

The first time I met Professor Dillman was at a seminar with him, Professor Wally Jay and Professor Remy Presas. My intention was to see and learn from Professor Wally Jay (as I had several of Professor Dillman's books and videos and quite frankly thought he was a little crazy!). Professor Presas was the first one to teach that day, and although I thoroughly enjoyed his session, I must admit that my closed-mindedness kept me from truly seeing his genius (this would change after I became a student of Professor Dillman's).

The next instructor was Professor Dillman, and right off the bat he began demonstrating moves out of kata that I had been doing for years, and dropping guys with applications that truly made sense. He had me sold until he tapped a guy and made him pass out. I did not believe this.

During the break between classes, I approached Professor Dillman and told him I enjoyed his session, but did not buy the whole "knockout thing." He proceeded to hit me on Stomach 5 and introduce my butt to the floor faster than any man had ever done. He asked me if I believed it now. My only response was, "Where do I sign up?"

◆ ◆ ◆ ◆ ◆

Several years ago, a group of many martial arts organizations got together and decided to promote Professor Dillman to Tenth Dan. He turned them down. When I asked him why, he told me that there were three things that he required to happen before he felt he was worthy of the rank.

- ◆ The first was that Professor Remy Presas and Wally Jay had either passed or were no longer teaching.

- ◆ Next was that Seiyu Oyata was no longer teaching.

- ◆ The third was that he had to be sixty-five years of age or older.

In 2008, a group of his peers and senior students got together and honored him with this promotion. This time he accepted.

◆ BILL BURCH, ILLINOIS, USA ◆

After a seminar in Ohio with Grandmaster Dillman, a bunch of us went to a famous bar to hear a great entertainer and have some fun for the evening. This particular establishment has a bar that winds over a mile in length! The singer draws a huge crowd every weekend, filling the building to capacity with fallout on the patio and the street. When the show ended we were all walking out, slowly crammed together like cattle trying to get outside. I was walking next to my brother for a while until we got outside and I noticed he wasn't next to me anymore. I looked back and saw that some big dude had him by the shirt, yelling to his girlfriend, "Is this the guy who was putting the moves on you?"

My brother was with us the entire night, and was now victim to some drunk who was just looking to beat someone up. I was trying to make my way back to him, like a salmon trying to swim upstream against the current. The drunk was about to take a swing at my brother when all of the sudden Grandmaster Dillman popped up next to the guy. "Excuse me," said Mr. Dillman as he grabbed the guy's ball cap, resting on top of his large cranium. He pulled the cap down tight across the guy's nose gave it a twist in two directions and then tapped him on the bridge of the nose with the heel of his palm. The dude dropped like he was tazed! His cap fell off and he started screaming "I can't see... I'm blind!" His girlfriend kept asking if he was okay. "I said I'm blind damn it... I can't see!" A block away, we could still hear him screaming: "I'm blind!"

Mr. Dillman explaining to us that before pressure points, he would have had a fight on his hands. Here, there was no blood or injury, except for this tough guy's image. His vision would return within twenty minutes or so, giving him just enough time to think about his attitude.

◆ JEFF BURHOP, ILLINOIS, USA ◆

This story takes place at the Shaolin Temple when Professor Dillman was demonstrating techniques in the cemetery grounds. Professor Dillman asked me to throw a front kick at him so he could demonstrate a technique for stopping my kick in midair before it struck him. I threw the front kick at Professor Dillman and he used his chi to stop it. I had never experienced this before! It felt like kicking 'hard air,' and it hurt my leg.

While I was still standing there and contemplating all of this, Professor Dillman must have assumed that I wanted to try it again, or maybe I didn't get the full effect, so he asked me to kick again. In doing what the Master asked, I kicked again, but this time Professor Dillman stepped forward to close the gap and entered my chi field to perform the technique. My kick was stopped again, but this time with much more force, like kicking a brick wall. It hurt bad! It took Master Steve Cooper three days of acupuncture treatments to get my knee and leg back in shape. It was, and still is, one of the most incredible things I have ever experienced in almost thirty years of training in martial arts...

◆ Dr. Ralph Buschbacher, Indiana, USA ◆

I have known George Dillman longer than most. I started in his class in 1971, when I was nine years old. We have traveled together, gone camping together, and taught many seminars together. I was his interpreter on the first seminars in Germany. I am a physician and showed him cadavers in medical school, and also gave him his first medical books.

I remember one particular sparring seminar in Virginia around 1985: There was a room of about thirty-five attendees along with George, Sandy, me and Kim. At least fifteen of the folks were advanced black belts. We were all sitting in a large circle and George started fighting one person after the other. The rounds were about two to three minutes long, so the whole thing took over an hour. I am not sure anyone even touched him in all those fights. He landed so many kicks and punches that it was impossible to count. He just rained those blows down on everyone, one after the other! It was truly impressive...

◆ S.C. Chan, New Zealand ◆

In 1985 my good friend and teacher, the venerable Professor Wally Jay, advised me that it would be in my interest to see a few special martial artists in the USA, with George Dillman on top of the list. When I first saw George Dillman, I did not know what to make of this brash American who made incredibly outrageous claims about classical Karate/Tae Kwon Do forms and their relationship with pressure points techniques. Even though I grew up in Asia knowing that pressure points techniques was supposed to be part of the higher levels of Kung Fu, I had never met anyone who could demonstrate it to me. I therefore thought that it was all totally lost, or greatly exaggerated.

Amazingly, George was able to back up his claims and demonstrate the effectiveness of pressure point techniques. It was particularly great to see him stun a known bully, who is an ugly giant of a man, with a tap, and leave him groggy for the rest of the seminar! It was one of the major turning points in my martial arts philosophy. I have since hosted his seminars and travelled to train with him, to see even more incredible developments of his knowledge and skills over the years.

Under his hard, uncompromising exterior, I found George to be a very sensitive, generous, and loyal friend and teacher. We had great fun and adventures on seminar tours in New Zealand and the USA. George Dillman is certainly one of the most important people that have greatly influenced my martial arts, and many others of our generation. Pressure points techniques just give so much more 'fire-power' and control to the martial artist using them. I will always be grateful to George.

◆ Tony Consentino, Pennsylvania, USA ◆

I started studying under Grandmaster Dillman in 1968 in Reading, Pennsylvania. We worked out at the Police Athletic League on Rose and Walnut Streets. Later we worked out at his Fifth Street dojo in Reading. I remember back then I saw pictures of George wrestling with a bear at different functions. Although I did not witness the event, I also heard of a challenge match between George and another black belt, in which the challenger ran away by crawling out a bathroom window!

There was a day when George had new contact lenses placed in his eyes. He mentioned right before a karate class that he was having trouble seeing clearly. Later in the class he asked me to spar with him. Noting that he was having vision problems, I was able to take advantage of this. When he threw a front kick at my mid-section, I was able to catch his foot and throw him to the ground and score a point. Instead of explaining to the class that his misfortune was due to his vision problems, he said: "Let that be a lesson not to underestimate your opponent!"

◆ STEVE COOPER, TENNESSEE, USA ◆

I remember the first time I met Grandmaster Dillman like it was yesterday. One of my jujutsu students said that Professor Wally Jay was going to be in Lexington, Kentucky for a seminar. He was double billing with Grandmaster George Dillman. Sensei Dillman got up first and said, "Every move in every kata is a killing move." I was immediately intrigued and wondered what kata he knew that were so deadly. Imagine my surprise when I found out they were the same ones that I knew. Well as the country song goes, he had me from "hello."

Life has not been the same since that day. I went home and couldn't sleep for two weeks. Every time I closed my eyes, all I saw was pressure points. I remember Professor Jay's teachings from that day very well, but Grandmaster Dillman's are burned in my mind forever. From that moment to this day, I have been a proud student of Grandmaster Dillman, and just as important as being my teacher, he is my friend.

◆ Gary Cunningham, Indiana, USA ◆

It was my good fortune that I was lucky enough to study under the "Big Three": Professor Wally Jay of Small Circle Jujitsu, Professor Remy Presas of Modern Arnis, and Professor George Dillman of Ryūkyū Kempo. Going against traditional, old school thinking, these great men encouraged cross-training and actually held seminars together, which was unheard of because most grandmasters were too insecure to share the limelight. Thanks to George Dillman's extensive research regarding pressure point theory, he has shared with the world the secrets of martial arts: the simple fact that every movement in kata represents a strike to a pressure point, or a grappling move to position an assailant to strike a pressure point. I credit George Dillman for showing me the correct path to reach my full potential as a martial artist.

◆ Allen Dillman, Pennsylvania, USA ◆

When I was approximately eighteen years old, I watched my father getting bored with martial arts. He thought that there was nothing left to learn or do. Then he learned of a man who was knocking people out by just touching them. I watched him rip apart every filing cabinet in our house for three days straight, until he found a set of notes that another man gave him twenty years earlier. He said that the second man had told him that these notes were the skills he was seeking, but he did not understand all of them. After watching the first man knock people out by touching them, he started to study the notes, and doing an in-depth study of the human body. I saw a whole new spark in my father's eyes that day, and still see it many years later.

◆ KIM DILLMAN, PENNSYLVANIA, USA ◆

PHOTO BY BOB HUBBARD
BOBHUBBARDPHOTOGRAPHY.COM

Travel was always in vogue from the time I began competition with the Dillman karate team until the divorce in 2004. George Dillman, I have always contended, is a gypsy at heart. It would have suited him to not have a house and live in an RV. I, on the other hand, wanted to put down roots with travel as necessary.

Traveling to karate tournaments began for me in 1969 when I went to my first competitive event in New York City at the Black Belt International Hall of Fame tournament in Manhattan. It was my first tournament and I took second place in forms as a yellow belt. I fought too, but in those days women's events were for all belt ranks and all levels of experience, so I didn't fare so well. In fact, I got my ass kicked pretty good, and limped home with black and blue shins, arms, and torso! I did, however, vow not to get so soundly trounced again. Yeah, sure—the hopes of a novice. This was where I first met such notables as Chuck Norris and Mike Stone.

From there we went on to travel throughout Pennsylvania, New Jersey, Maryland, Virginia, Ohio, Indiana, North Carolina, Connecticut, Massachusetts, New York, Canada and eventually to California. During 1970 and 1971, I went on to win hundreds of trophies in form, fighting, and weapons. Dillman at this time was competing in tandem with his students and was considered one of the top competitors in the U.S.

We were so into competition that it was not unusual to hit two tournaments in one weekend. I remember driving through the night in Dillman's station wagon to Asheville, North Carolina, arriving at 3:30 in the morning to compete in a tournament on Saturday morning at 10:00 and then taking off for Virginia that night to compete in a tournament on Sunday near Richmond, Virginia. Bear in mind that the interstate highway system was not yet fully finished, so there were a lot of wrong turns on back roads at night to get to our destinations. Sleep was a luxury then. I could not even think about doing this today. But we were all young, foolish, and highly motivated to make our mark in the history of American martial arts.

Soon after this, Dillman acquired his first RV, which made road trips a little easier, except that as many students that could find sleeping space were piled into the RV. Life on the road was as challenging as the tournaments we competed in. We had one bathroom, and took our showers in the gyms when they were available. If not, we stank or rigged a hose and blankets at a roadside rest. Food on the road was not highly nutritious: sandwiches, cereal, and lots of beer and soda. But we had fun. We often left at night when it was cooler since the RV didn't have air-conditioning, and arrived at our destination in the very early morning. That old eight-track tape player got a workout, and we all knew the words to all of the songs of The Four Tops, Smokey Robinson, Elvis Presley, Elton John, and The Carpenters. Maybe that's where my love of karaoke got started, I don't know. The early 70's are a blur of weekends in the RV, traveling to tournaments and seminars. Once I started college, my competition days were curtailed by study and time, but the team motored on. By then I was tired of getting bruised anyway, so I was happy to send them off on a trip and mind the dojo back home.

The summer I graduated from college, Dillman sold his only vehicle, a jeep, and bought a nineteen foot Jamboree RV. We took off on a trip around the US in that little thing. Two other students went along: Mark Kopcick and Sandy Schlessman. We had over a month to kill and we took the scenic route, starting a Mike Patton's tournament in Ohio and continuing across the country on the northern route. Chicago was fun to drive through. Yes, anytime there was a lot of traffic to contend with, I seemed to get the chore of driving. Somehow, Dillman always needed a nap. "Just stay on 90 and wake me when we are out of town."

Folks, the Great Plains are really the great pains when you drive for hours across vast fields of corn and wheat. I know, this is the heartland of America, but at the time, I ached for hills and trees, roads that had a little bend and curve to break the monotony. We got into South Dakota and stopped to visit with a former student who was stationed there. We explored the Badlands and Mount Rushmore and checked out Deadwood before all the casinos, before heading west into Colorado and then Wyoming. I was grateful for the mountains: the fresh, cool air, the scents of sage, pines and smoking campfires in the dew of a brisk morning. The wonders of Yellowstone National Park and its sulfurous mud pots and thundering geysers, its many various animals, and the Grand Canyon of the Yellowstone are scenes that I will never forget. We stayed there for several days before heading out again to Jackson Hole and onward.

We cut south and continued west into Utah and across the great salt flats—mercifully at night. I was at the wheel for that drive, and it was the night of a full moon. The moonlight on the vast whiteness of the salt flats was beautiful, and even though it was fully night, it was almost like driving during that hour of dusk when the sun isn't fully up and yet not fully down. We moved on into Nevada stopping in Las Vegas, which at that time was relatively small. The strip wasn't that big, but the lights were bright, and the shows and casinos beckoned. We camped at the Frontier Hotel campground, gambled in their casino, went to the Rodney Dangerfield show, and followed him to his favorite blackjack table afterward.

There is no way I could stay up that late or sleep in so late any more, especially since it was August in Las Vegas and we had no air-conditioning. The second night there we were to go to Wayne Newton, but our tickets weren't held. Instead of the show, we walked the strip, ate a wonderful but cheap dinner at one of the hotels, and went back to the Frontier Casino. Drinks were free as long as you fed the one-armed bandits, and penny and nickel slots fit my budget and that of the others. Sandy borrowed a dollar from Mark and promptly hit for $50. Mark tried to claim the $50, but got only $1 back. Sandy's debt was repaid in full as far as she was concerned.

Since it was already late, Sandy and I decided to crash for the night to get some sleep while it was still relatively cool. Dillman and Mark decided to stay and play a little longer. It was shortly after Sandy and I left that they met Johnny Cash in the men's room, and were asked to join him at shooting craps. I remember Dillman being amazed at the stack of chips Cash was holding from various casinos all over town. "Must've had fifty-thou in chips. I sure would have liked to have played some of those."

The trip continued westward to Los Angeles. I remember driving, again at night, over the crest of a mountain and seeing nothing but lights in the distance. Mark and Dillman were sleeping and Sandy and I gasped out loud at the view. We woke them up to see the sight, and at the next view point, I pulled over to take in the view. I am sure we looked like the biggest rubes in the world to the passing motorists and truckers, but quite frankly, we didn't care. I made coffee while we gawked at the lights, and armed with caffeine, we moved on, down into the sea of lights and right into the heart of tinsel town.

I remember parking in the lot of a theatre on Hollywood Boulevard early in the morning and crawling into my bunk while the morning rush traffic swooshed and honked outside. Again, sleep was a novelty, and after a few hours we filled with water from a nearby faucet, showered and went out to explore Sunset Boulevard, Mann's Chinese Theatre, the Capitol Building, and the stars on the walk of fame. Later that morning we found our way to Burbank and to the offices of *Black Belt* magazine, where Dillman and I were interviewed for an article.

We then had lunch at a Mexican restaurant nearby before returning to our parking lot in Hollywood. You could get away with parking at hotels back then. Security wasn't what it is now. In fact, we had used the parking lots of various hotels and grocery stores while making our way across the US. We used their pools, exchanged dirty towels for clean—the maids were always generous—hooked up to their water and filled out tanks, all for free. Sure beat paying for campgrounds every night. We only did that when we needed to empty the black and gray water. Now you wouldn't get away with any of that, without being a paying guest. Such was the simple life of the 1970s in America.

Ryūkyū Kempo

That evening we walked to the karate school of Tak Kubota, watched his class and then introduced ourselves. He knew of Dillman and we were then asked to perform kata for him. Other than that, I don't remember much of that night since we lower ranks were not important enough to be part of the conversation. We went back to the RV and some rest before heading out in the morning.

It was now mid-August and time to head east. We traveled across Interstate 10 to Phoenix Arizona to visit with Robert Trias, the founder and head of the USKA. After some time, we found his dojo, and watched while he finished up a class. Trias had a dynamometer in his dojo. We watched several of his black belts test out their punch power on it. Dillman asked if, after class, we could have a go. Well, we did and it became a sort of competition between Dillman, Sandy, me and Trias' black belts. After a few tries, we discovered that proper body dynamics and intent were the most important things to really deliver a powerful punch. We had been taught "flow" or intent by Daniel K. Pai and we put his teachings to work that night. By then end of the ad hoc competition, Sandy and I had out powered two of Trias' black belts. They were sorely abused by their classmates, and we remained unapologetic. That night ended in a pool hall not far from Trias' dojo where the beer was cold, and the tacos were deliciously hot! We were allowed to camp in the parking lot of the USKA headquarters, and the next morning we set out to explore some of Phoenix. We got to the zoo, and looked around downtown before hitting the road into New Mexico.

Crossing New Mexico and Texas on Interstate 10 was as much of a pain as were the plains. It seemed like forever before we got into the high country of Texas before dropping down into San Antonio. There we got a camp ground and Dillman called an old friend of his mother's family with whom we visited for a day. It was there that I learned that the fruit of the prickly pear cactus was delicious to eat, but deadly to peel. I also learned the trick to that, and how to make prickly pear jelly.... Yum! Every time I see cactus apples for sale in the grocery store, my fingers hurt, but my mouth waters.

We headed out the other side of Texas through Houston and on into Louisiana and New Orleans. The Big Easy provided us with a nice shady parking spot next to a boarded up restaurant, within walking distance of the French Quarter. It was like walking into a foreign country. The sights and the sounds of New Orleans jazz blended with the spices of Creole food and rum concoctions will never fade away. We wanted to eat at Chez Paul's, but since Dillman and Mark didn't have ties, we were refused entry. Of course, they could have rented them, but we opted for Po'boys at a little mom-and-pop eatery around the corner from the RV.

Continuing our way east, we crossed into Mississippi and Alabama before turning north. By now time was running out, and we needed to make a run for Pennsylvania. I remember driving northward through the night, following a Piggly Wiggly truck, winding through the hills of Tennessee and listening to country music since we could get nothing else on the radio (funny, back then I detested country music; now I listen to it all the time. One of Dillman's sons joked that "listening to country is a product of age." I wonder if he now listens to country since he is now well "aged" himself). I pulled off at a rest stop in the early hours of a morning near Knoxville to catch some rest to awaken to a breathtaking view of the Appalachians and the scent of wild grapes in the air.

The last leg was a cruise through the mountains of Virginia and the Blue Ridge Parkway. Little did we know then that we would be visiting that area more frequently as Dillman Karate picked up a few schools in that region. I remember honking the horn of the RV when we crossed the Pennsylvania state line just above Hagerstown, Maryland. In another three hours we would be home in Reading.

◆ SUZANNE JOHN DILLMAN, READING, USA ◆

I actually miss traveling for seminars. I got to travel all over the world with George, and when the seminars were over, we would go sight-seeing. Some of my favorite places to visit were Yosemite in the United States, and the UK. One place I'd still like to see is Costa Rica—for the birds!

Ryūkyū Kempo

◆ Greg Dillon, Indiana, USA ◆

Having had the privilege of studying and traveling with Sensei Dillman throughout the US and abroad for twenty five years, I have seen how he has changed the way the martial arts world approaches kata and self-defense. Whether working with law enforcement, the military or women's self-defense, the actual hand-to-hand situations can be adapted anywhere. What was once just theory is now an intentionally accredited program. George Dillman is truly a martial arts pioneer.

◆ Hernan Fung, Costa Rica ◆

Sensei, I think if you were Japanese, Chinese, or Korean, you would be more renowned than Gichin Funakoshi or Jigoro Kano (not to say that you aren't famous)! We, the people, know that no other martial artist has been able to extract the hidden secrets of the martial arts and make them available to everyone so that they can make their techniques ten thousand times more powerful—only you have done that. And if the stories of ancient masters defeating younger, stronger opponents are true, they most certainly used pressure points. This is the truth.

◆ Keith Gray, UK ◆

My first meeting with George Dillman was, to be brutally honest, something I expected to see in the movies from the Far East, where ninja masters jump off buildings and are actually immortal. Thanks to my instructor, Paul Bowman, I decided to attend a seminar in Epsom, England held by Leon Jay of Small Circle fame. As I walked into the seminar, I could see lots of karate men in their gis. To me at the time karate was an art you practiced to learn self-defence badly.

At the time I had just retired at the age of 35 after a fighting career of 85 full contact fights and 7 years on the door as a bouncer. As my instructor Paul Bowman was only 5'4" and a real force to be reckoned with, he had impressed me enough to attend on the day. The whole seminar was a blur to me as I was seeing things I never dreamt possible. Toward the end of the day, George Dillman was walking around a large group of people, striking with the palm of his hand on the side of their face. At the time I was thinking, "Why are those guys sitting on the floor he hardly touched them?" Then he approached me.

To this day I thought he was going to strike me. So I waited to see what happened. He placed his hands approximately three inches for my head then all of a sudden—without touching me—I found myself sitting down. People asked me afterwards what did that feel like. My reply was it felt like I was a little baby, no responsibilities, no worries—karma comes to mind. Sixteen years later the rest is history.

◆ Deborah Grimaldi, Illinois, USA ◆

I remember when I first joined DKI and was fired up. One day I was talking to George and then the next thing I knew, there he was at my school. He drove fourteen hours to be there. When he arrived, he just started teaching. I had the children's class, then the junior class and then the adult class; he taught for over four hours. When the last class was over, all the students wanted his autograph and every student stayed. I'm sure my students then called up the students that didn't get to class that day because they also showed up! It was great! Thank you George.

◆ Matt Hayat, Maryland, USA ◆

Ryūkyū Kempo

I was at Grandmaster Dillman's Toronto seminar in 2003. I am hard of hearing; I *do* hear, just not well at times. I had been teaching a system combining Dillman Method techniques with American Sign Language phrases and words. Near the end of the seminar that Saturday afternoon, Grandmaster Dillman introduced me to the large crowd of 100+ martial arts practitioners, and gave me fifteen minutes or so to demonstrate some Martial Signs, as well as giving the seminar attendees a chance to try them. While introducing me, he said, "this is Matt Hayat, he's deaf and can't hear you when you talk to him so you have to use your hands," and then he made a couple of quick gestures with his hands. After the seminar ended, I was standing near the doorway where all of these people were exiting. They thought I was totally deaf and couldn't hear! Many participants came up to me and motioned with their hands and mouthed praise very dramatically, saying that they liked the techniques I shared. Pretty funny—I kept saying, "I can hear you just fine!"

◆ JOE HAMMOND, VERMONT, USA ◆

I remember attending a George Dillman sparring clinic in White River Junction, Vermont many years ago. Master Dillman showed up with his pet cougar and a few of his black belts. The clinic started off with everyone sparring with one of Master Dillman's black belts. Most of us understood that next we would be fighting George himself, and it would be unwise to unload on his student because we would pay for it when we fought George. One student after another engaged in controlled, light sparring with George's students until it came to one black belt who put some real heat on George's student and then sat down, obviously pleased with himself.

When George sparred everyone there, things went smooth until it came to the black belt who had really gone after his student. George bounced him off the walls, mopped the floor with him, and then instructed him to sit down. George continued sparring with the rest of the students present in a controlled manner.

◆ WILL HIGGINBOTHAM, INDIANA, USA ◆

I remember my first meeting with George Dillman well. We were introduced by the host of the seminar he was about to teach in Terre Haute, Indiana.

He said, "Do you do this move in your kata training?" It was a double knife hand block.

I said "Yes."

He said, "Would you use it in a real fight?"

I said, "No."

"Why," he asked?

I said, "Because it would be too slow to stop the punch as a block."

He said, "Right, what if it meant this? Throw a punch."

I said, "I can punch pretty fast."

He said, "That's OK, I can move pretty fast!"

Ryūkyū Kempo

I punched at his head and he struck my forearm with the first half of the move and my neck with the second half of the move. The next thing I knew, he was slapping me on the back of the head and I was waking up. I knew I had been knocked out and I said, "Yeah, I'd use it like that!" At that point, the hook was set and I knew I had to train with him to learn what karate was really about.

❖ ❖ ❖ ❖ ❖

He's one of the most entertainingly funny instructors I have ever met. His seminars are always serious, but laced with comedy. I pity all the people that don't get to know the personal side of George Dillman. He comes across as hard-edged, sarcastic and always humorous, but he is truly one of the most generous and compassionate human beings I know. When I went through my divorce, he called me every day to see how I was doing. He would try to pump me up and make me feel good about myself. He would always close with, "We love ya', baby!"

The night before a seminar years ago I was invited to George's hotel room where several of us had pizza and beer and conversation. When the evening came to an end he asked me and my student to take the rest of the pizza with us. As we were leaving the room he said, "If you throw the crumbs out on the lawn instead of throwing them in the trash, the birds will love ya'." He was always thinking in favor of animals and their welfare.

❖ **STERLING JOHNSON, VIRGINIA, USA** ❖

I first met George Dillman when he was doing his "farewell" karate tournaments. I was fourteen years old. It was very exciting to watch him do his kata. Later I got to ask him questions because my karate instructor was not with me all the time. I asked him, "What do I need to do to become a winner like you? Could you watch me fight and tell me what I need to work on?" When I grow up I want to be just like George.

♦ Esti Laaksonen, Finland ♦

In 1993, I gave a lecture on human anatomy at one of George Dillman's martial arts seminars. I recall that the place was packed with people and I had the chance to observe various fights, knockouts and other examples of nerve point contacts. This all was very interesting. We travelled to many places with George and Kim. One of these places was Muhammad Ali's training camp that George had just purchased. George is a very good story teller and he made us laugh many times. One day George invited me and my husband Tero to eat turkey at his and Kim's place. George told us that turkey is very good food because it makes you sleepy. Five minutes after we heard snoring at the sofa. Tero had fallen asleep!

♦ Tero Laaksonen, Finland ♦

In 1991, George and Kim Dillman held a seminar in Finland. It was their biggest seminar abroad with 200 participants, some of whom had come from other Nordic countries. I remember George being amazed of how a small country like Finland could host a seminar of such magnitude (Finland's population is 5.2 million). The host of the seminar was my martial arts mentor, Mr. Ilpo Jalamo. The participants wished to test the efficiency of the previously unworkable techniques and Mr. Big-D (George Dillman), which the Finnish budo-press had nicknamed him, knocked out to the twilight zone nearly seventy martial artists from various styles.

In 1998 the Dillmans and I made a three-seminar tour of Sweden and Finland. Göteborg was our first stop and George presented his skills to practitioners of Krav Maga and kickboxing. We continued by train along a beautiful trail to Stockholm, Sweden's capital. Professor Wally Jay had followed that same route a few years before us. At the Stockholm seminar I saw George doing a back of a hand knock-out to the ear for the first time. Moments after, there was a freezer-sized martial artist on my lap. After several years of studying and teaching acupuncture I have come to understand better what it was all about.

Ryūkyū Kempo

A year after the Stockholm seminar, I was teaching my own seminar and made a hit with a special-fist to the ear. As a result of this, the person on the receiving end lost his sight for a moment. He was standing quite close to me, but couldn't see a thing. He later told me the situation had been frightening, as if he had been watching a TV that showed only a blur and no picture. I have shared numerous moments and laughs with George in the 1990s, even a part of which would alone fill this book.

◆ ED LAKE, NEVADA, USA ◆

It was during the winter of 1989 that I finally got a chance to host a Dillman seminar. I had been to every dojo in South Miami and found a Tai Chi man to host a Thursday night seminar. I was very nervous because this was my first real seminar with Mr. Dillman. Well the seminar started as it always did by talking about World War II and how we had occupied Japanese islands and how the Japanese did not want to teach us real karate. And, as always, Mr. Dillman controlled the seminar in his most professional manner.

As he explained why pressure points were never brought to America, some of the higher ranking masters in the room started looking nervous due to the fact that none of them knew anything about what he was talking about. But there was this one in particular—a third degree black belt—who was listening intensely to Mr. Dillman and hung on every word that he said.

After the seminar we went to eat at a Cuban restaurant in South Miami and stood in the parking lot until six o'clock in the morning talking about karate, keeping Mr. Dillman out very late. The next morning after we woke up I got told phone call from a one of the participants from the seminar.

He had just gotten off the phone with the third degree black belt who gone to his karate instructor's house at three o'clock in the morning demanding his money back for the last eighteen years because he did not teach him "real karate."

♦ SHANE LEAR, OHIO, USA ♦

I attended the trip to China with Grandmaster Dillman and many other martial artists from across the world in September of 2006. This trip was historic in the sense that Grandmaster Dillman was taking karate back to its original roots at the Shaolin Temple. I can truly say that this trip changed my life completely. For the next few years after our return, I had heard that there were plans to build a relationship with Shaolin for the future and the possibility of the monks training martial artists in DKI. I decided that it was my duty to help Grandmaster Dillman with this endeavor.

In April of 2009, I spent a month in China training six hours per day in Kung Fu, Qigong, Tai Chi, pressure points and energetics. The contacts that I was able to attain on this trip have allowed me to assist with Grandmaster Dillman's goal. In September of 2010, I arranged the first training group for this purpose. The group spent seven days training in Kung Fu and Qigong with two monks directly inside the Shaolin Temple. During this trip we also had the honor of meeting the head abbot of the Temple: Shi Yongxin. We discussed many things, including training principles and the cultural experience of Shaolin. I also had the honor of delivering a letter from Grandmaster Dillman to Shi Yongxin. This letter contained information related to the future of DKI and Shaolin. This trip has enabled DKI to begin a relationship directly with the Temple for future trips and eventually a dedication to Grandmaster Dillman and DKI commemorated in the historic Shaolin Temple garden.

Ryūkyū Kempō

I would like to thank Grandmaster Dillman for everything that he has done for the martial arts community and for myself. Through his many efforts, he has laid the groundwork that will enable future generations to discover the true essence of the martial arts.

◆ Phil LeBash, Pennsylvania, USA ◆

I had been trained in the martial arts by Master George Dillman and the late Pai Lum Hawaiian Martial Arts Master Daniel Pai. I remember a time back in 1970 at a National Karate Tournament in Washington D.C. I was a witness of a disagreement between the late legendary film martial artist Bruce Lee and George Dillman, I must say there was no physical contact, but George Dillman does not back down from anyone and he can hold his own with any other famous martial artist. Kudos goes out to Master George Dillman for showing the world the many ways the martial arts can enlighten a person's life.

◆ Chuck Lentz, Pennsylvania, USA ◆

George had just discovered Oyata. He divulged to a group of his black belts that something had happened that brought everything he had learned into focus. He instantly began to change his teaching style to include this new knowledge. This proved frightening to some of the students as size and power developed through sparring training no longer meant physical dominance. Speed and accuracy guided by this new understanding of pressure points had completely altered what was good self-defense. The study of kata and their bunkai was now what was most important.

At the time George remembered an old notebook a grandmaster had given him with the words, "Everything you need to know is in here." George told us that he looked at it and it did not seem to make sense to him at the time. Ideas like, "Touch here with this knuckle and unconsciousness will occur." George thought, "Why not hit the spot with your whole fist, with power?" So he told us that he put the notebook away and forgot about it until Oyata brought pressure points back into focus.

◆ Dr. Harvey Levy, Maryland, USA ◆

I have trained in the martial arts since I was a fifteen year-old boy in Brooklyn, New York. At age sixty-one, I reflect upon my most memorable martial arts experience, which happened at a DKI training camp in 2004. After some introductions, Grandmaster Dillman talked about light-touch and no-touch knock-outs. Some of us in the room had heard about them and read about them, but never seen or experienced them. Grandmaster Dillman introduced everyone to Canada's Steve Stewart, who then proceeded to perform several jaw-dropping no-touch knock-outs from ten yards away. I videotaped the whole thing, and that weekend I witnessed several more light- and no-touch knock-outs by Stewart and others.

After camp I returned home, and showed the videos to my girlfriend (now my wife). She is a scientist, a physicist and a skeptic. She thought I had doctored the video, which she proceeded to rewind and review more than fifty times. She then declared that she had to see this for herself. Lena, who grew up in a traditional judo home in Sao Paulo, Brazil, joined me for the next two DKI camps, and experienced this impossible phenomenon for herself. She trained hard, earned a green belt, and used her new-found light-touch knock-out skills to daze men twice her weight. Lena the skeptic was now Lena the believer and advocate of this illogical, implausible, yet here-it-is phenomenon.

A kayaking injury forced Lena to stop training, but I continue to train with Grandmaster George Dillman and Grandmaster Chris Thomas, having attended over twenty of their weekend training camps. Although I hold a third degree in Tang Soo Do and Senior Instructor certificate in Combat Hapkido, I still train twice a week with my Maryland DKI and KJK groups. I am the owner of the HarLen Martial Arts Club in Keedysville, Maryland, and have been a proud and active DKI affiliate school of Grandmaster George Dillman for over five years.

I am passionate about the martial arts, an important journey in my life; they have taught me many lessons, such as perseverance and discipline. Both my daughters earned black belts at about the time they graduated high school. They feel capable of protecting themselves against some of the risks lurking in the streets of life, and I feel thankful for having contributed to that.

I am also grateful to George Dillman for helping me make sense of memorized kata, and for giving dimension to the bunkai. Without understanding of their meaning and applications, kata are just pretty, choreographed dances, which would only be truly useful if attacked by a ballerina! I continue to enjoy and appreciate the journey and Grandmaster George Dillman, who has been an integral mentor and role model.

◆ COTTON MARKS, CALIFORNIA, USA ◆

The first time I met George Dillman was in 2001 at a *Black Belt* magazine photo shoot. George bought everybody lunch that day, so that night I went to pay for his dinner without him knowing. I will never forget what he said to me once he found out:

"Do you know who I am and what I do for a living?"

I replied, "Yes, I do know who you are and I know you can kick my ass, but I am still paying for your dinner."

We have had a great friendship ever since. One of the things that impressed me the most about George is that it doesn't matter to him who you are or what rank you are, but what does matter is your character and willingness to learn and to share what you have learned.

◆ MARK MARSHALL, OHIO, USA ◆

It was October 1992. We were in Jacksonville, Florida for a "Big Three" Seminar. The Big Three of course were Grandmaster Wally Jay, Grandmaster Remy Presas and Grandmaster George Dillman. Our host was Jack Hogan. During this time, George referred to a group of us individually as his "best buddy"[9] Not "best buddie**s**," but singularly, as if each were the only one. Mark Kline took this one step further and made T-shirts that proclaimed the wearer as George Dillman's Best Buddy. I still have the T-shirt and wear it occasionally to seminars.

At the end of the day, we enjoyed a huge banquet. There must have been two or three hundred people attendance. The "Best Buddies" arrived with jackets covering our shirts. Jack Hogan was at the lectern thanking everyone for coming and making the seminar a success. He continued to

---

[9] Those with an eye for detail will recognize that a peculiarly Okinawan term for "best buddy" is: *Kubichiridushi*...

say that the most rewarding thing was the he knew that he was George's best buddy; that all weekend long, George referred to him as his "best buddy." And of all the people George knew, that he was number one.

After a few minutes of this, Kim Foreman, who was George's wife at the time, stood up and said the she was George's wife, and if anyone was his "best buddy," it was her. After a few minutes of squabbling, Kim said that if she were not his best buddy, then why did he give her a T-shirt proclaiming such. She unzipped her jacket to expose the Best Buddy T-shirt. At that moment, Jack said the same thing and exposed his Best Buddy T-shirt. Then the rest of us stood up saying, "Hey he gave us T-shirts also!" The crowd erupted in laughter.

George sat there stunned. George, the man who was always telling jokes and pulling practical jokes, had a practical joke pulled on him. If he did not realize it before, George knew now that we were truly one big family.

◆ DAVID MARTIN, UK ◆

Whilst here in the UK doing a seminar visit in 2006, myself and other UK DKI representatives, including Grandmaster Paul Bowman, accompanied Mr. Dillman on a visit and sight-seeing trip to London. Whilst we visited the Tower of London museum and walked the grounds Professor Dillman, in his normal light-hearted manner, decided to stand and generate his chi energy towards one of the sentry guards in full dress uniform that are not allowed to be distracted or move. The guardsman could not understand why he was compelled to sway and almost stagger forward!

That evening whilst travelling back on the underground train Professor Dillman decided to play this trick again and this time a very confused man wondered which of his pockets to look in next for something. I am not sure what he was looking for and I do not think he did either but it was hard to keep a straight face watching this poor chap constantly checking all of his trouser and coat pockets aware he was doing it but could not stop. Always playing, but harmless fun...

♦ David Melton, Oklahoma, USA ♦

Life can be rewarding or not depending upon those around you. My interests in life and my rewards have come from my commitments, studies of my spiritual life, my thirty-three career that I have been passing on to others through my school to try and enhance their lives, and my artistic life, which has been mainly centered around the martial arts and music since I was a kid. I have had the good fortune to have studied with very talented and well-known and respected people who helped me grow in these areas of my life, of which I have tried hard to be an ambassador to them as a way of expressing my eternal gratitude and respect to them.

Grandmaster Dillman, in my travels and journeys I have expressed what I believe is a rare gift to others I have met while in their dojo, and that is being able to demonstrate to a group of strangers what you have so graciously provided me. I leave their dojo with a real since of pride that I'm associated with one of the best ever in these arts. I've learned that being a teacher is a great reward because it takes real dedication, compassion, and devotion. Thank you for your dedication, devotion and compassion. I'm very proud to be one of your students and friends. I wish you and your family the very best.

◆ GARY McKENNEY, VERMONT, USA ◆

I have been a member of the DKI since the mid-seventies, before the pressure point era. I earned my first DKI rank in 1976 under Sensei Joseph Hammond but did not meet then-Master Dillman until October 27th of 1979. The occasion was a tournament-style sparring clinic hosted by Sensei Peter Porter at his dojo in White River Junction, Vermont.

My instructor and I arrived early and joined a group of 20+ karate practitioners of various styles who were also awaiting George's arrival. Having only seen photos of Master Dillman I had an idea of his physical appearance and turned my attention to the main entrance when word passed through the room that Master Dillman was about to enter. I have to admit that my first reaction was surprise given his rank and accomplishments that he was about 5' 10"—only an inch or so taller than me—and not a much larger man. I guess I really had expected a "larger-than-life" figure to be the Master of DKI. My first impression was to change quite quickly.

George moved to the center of the room and instructed us to sit in a large circle. He gave a brief introduction of his background and achievements in the martial arts and confirmed the topic of the clinic. He went on to say that there were usually some doubters at clinics like these, and that he would address that concern immediately by sparring everyone in the room before beginning his instructional session. A silence fell across the room at the prospect of sparring the head of the DKI and George wasted no time in calling up his first opponent—me!

I was a brown belt at the time and, as I stated earlier, about the same size as Master Dillman. With one of his personal students serving as referee, we were instructed to assume the fighting position and the command to begin was issued. I immediately launched a spinning technique which I thought was certain to impress George with my speed and dexterity. He nodded approvingly, and with renewed confidence I returned to the fighting position with the intention of further impressing him with my abilities. Wrong!

At the command to fight, George stepped in, grabbed my left wrist with his left hand, pulled it across my chest, and launched a right hand punch that stopped just short of my nose. It was so fast that I didn't move from the position I was standing in. George smiled, stepped back, and reassumed his fighting position.

Once again the command to fight was given, and the same technique resulted in the same outcome. Again, I never moved from my fighting stance. Again, George just smiled and returned to his fighting stance. I decided to allow a bit more room between us as I prepared for the next encounter, to give myself time to react to George's speed. Unfortunately, this tactic was useless as George repeated his attack for the third time and achieved the same result. Despite several years of experience in the martial arts at that time, I was completely unprepared for the hand speed of Master Dillman.

Our 'match' ended and I returned, somewhat embarrassed, to my place in the circle as the next opponent was called upon to spar with Master Dillman. The variety of styles called for George to vary his tactics, but it was apparent to everyone in the room that he was more than up to the challenge of facing all the participants at the clinic. A few opponents attacked more aggressively and this just seemed to raise George's sparring to another level as he met the challenges with a level of aggressiveness he seemed to reserve for such encounters.

Having conclusively dispatched each participant George simply said, "Now we can begin the clinic." To this day I cannot remember encountering another martial artist with the hand speed of George Dillman.

Since that clinic in 1979 I have sponsored or attended seminars by Grandmaster Dillman on sparring, kata performance, breaking, and of course, pressure point techniques. Still, the one that has made the most lasting impression on me was the one at which I experienced, up close and personal, the hand speed of Grandmaster Dillman.

◆ JOSH MOREE, ATLANTA, USA ◆

After studying traditional martial arts for some time, I had been at seminars and training sessions where masters and grandmasters of various styles were present. Notice I didn't say I "met" them, because lowly kyu ranks or first degree black belts were generally not allowed to talk to the higher ranks.

It was in 2003 that I first met George Dillman at a seminar in Nashville, Tennessee. The first thing I noticed was that when he walked into the room, he shook the hand of everyone there and thanked them for coming. Such as small gesture left a huge impact on me in my personal training, my perception of those who are willing to share knowledge, and also how I approach others now wishing to learn from me. There are a few encounters in my martial arts past that are mile markers, that is one of them.

◆ ROSE & CHUCK MOWERY, PENNSYLVANIA, USA ◆

While Grandmaster Dillman was on his Spring Tour during May of 1997, there was an article about Muhammad Ali's training camp being up for sale in the local newspaper. Previously, he had told us stories of training with Muhammad Ali, being at the camp, and the offer that Mr. Ali had made to him at that time. Since I was in daily contact with Grandmaster Dillman due to my responsibilities as his student for maintaining the business in his absence, I informed him of the article and kept it for him.

Upon his return, Grandmaster Dillman contacted Mr. Ali and the realtor and arranged to visit the camp. We drove him there. It was raining when we arrived, and when we got out of the vehicle, the weeds and grass all over the camp were up to our waists. Grandmaster Dillman, however, immediately saw the potential of the historic camp and made an offer. By July of that same year, we were driving to settlement with Grandmaster Dillman at the same restaurant where he and Muhammad Ali first met. And the rest, as they say, is history.

◆ JOHN RALSTON, VIRGINIA, USA ◆

To get the full scope of my time with Grandmaster George A. Dillman, I must first talk about Grandmaster Ed Lake. I had been studying martial arts for about nine years. I had reached brown belt in Goju-Ryu Karate before becoming something of a "dojo gypsy." A friend at the time was teaching at a school called "The Black Belt Factory" (no lie!). He had heard about a seminar. He would not be able to make it until the end since he was teaching that day, and asked if I would go so he could get a better idea of the material presented. I agreed, and on the day in question, I signed in and went to the locker room to change into my gi.

While changing, I heard a voice say, "How are you doing? I'm Ed Lake." I introduced myself and he asked about my style and what kata I did. "Goju-Ryu? They have a really cool bow. What's your bunkai?" he asked. I passed on the impractical explanation I had been taught. "Well, that's something. Want to see a different meaning?" I said I did and then "the lights went out." I was on the ground and Ed was waking me up. I had just been knocked out with the bow of my kata. He did not even hit me really. He just tapped me on the body. It was not the classical boxers "KO" on the jaw. I said to myself, "Okay, this is something I need to learn."

That is how I became a student of Grandmaster George Dillman. In a way, I met him that day, as this was something of a tradition: Ed's teacher had KO'd him in much the same way, with a bunkai from kata, and

Grandmaster Dillman had similar experiences with the legendary Hohan Soken and Grandmaster Seiyu Oyata. It is a tradition I am happy to be a part of. That day changed not only the direction of my martial arts but also my life.

I met the man himself the following year, after studying with Grandmaster Lake and watching most of the Dillman videotapes. We were already noticing some of his mannerisms and expressions. My training partner's daughter was well acquainted with his voice; as an infant she would often fall asleep to the sound of it. One night at a seminar in Jacksonville, Florida, there was a little "meet and greet" before the training sessions started. The Grandmasters had all of their books, videotapes, and tee-shirts out, and were signing autographs and chatting with attendees. I walked up to Grandmaster Dillman and asked him to sign my book. I had purchased the copy years earlier, and the glue in the binding hadn't held up to my constant reading. When pages started to come loose, I had it drilled so it would fit in a three-ring binder. He looked at me as if I had a third eye for a second before saying, "What did you do to my book?" I felt like I had just insulted him. But, he just smiled at me good naturedly and shook my hand. "Careful when you shake Wally's hand," he warned me and signed my book.

He then gave me another look and shook his head at me. "Your Ryukyu Kempo patch is upside down. Oyata wrote that out for me you know." Now terribly embarrassed, I decided to ask to take a picture with me and my then-girlfriend. He heartily agreed and snapped a picture with his hand on my shoulder, smiling broadly. When my now-wife's turn came, he got in close to her. Cheek-to-cheek with that same smile, he said to me, "What are you going to do?" Without thinking I blurted out, "Find your wife!" I think it was at this point he decided I was okay. I could take a little ribbing and respond. His sense of humor throughout DKI is legendary. I recall stories of the crank calls that went on between the upper ranks and Grandmaster Dillman himself.

I had the honor of being a guest in the Dillman home a few times, initially to help Grandmaster Ed Lake make the long drive from Miami, Florida, to Reading, Pennsylvania. While I was there, I got to see his Seventh Dan diploma from Oyata and the razor-sharp sword he used for demonstrations. I visited the location of his original school and trained at the current one at the time. I was able to visit the Muhammed Ali Training Camp when he first bought it, even before he had invested in remodeling and upkeep. He gave us the grand tour, recounting many stories of his time there with the Champ and other celebrities. He talked about plans for a grand martial arts training center. This was a plan he ultimately fulfilled.

I was also there for the medical study he conducted at the University of Pennsylvania in 1996. I was introduced to his first instructor, Harry Smith. I recall eating at a restaurant while he was teaching a group of us at the dinner table about breaking and energy projection. To demonstrate, he asked the waiter for a raw potato. The waiter looked at him oddly, but complied. The Grandmaster held the potato between the thumb and forefinger of his left hand and picked up a straw with the right hand. He then threw the straw at the potato and pierced it clean through to the other side! It was impressive to say the least.

Over the years, I have gotten to spend a lot of time with Grandmaster Dillman. In addition to being a top-notch martial artist and instructor, he has always been the consummate host, making sure everyone is having a good time, sharing the best items on the menu, and always having a great story to keep the conversation lively. I have been his student and friend now for almost thirty years, and am look forward to the next thirty!

◆ ANDREW REESE, PENNSYLVANIA, USA ◆

I started my martial arts journey back in 1968 at a downtown YMCA facility in Grand Forks, North Dakota. I was the biggest kid in fourth grade: 5'8" tall. I was even taller than my teacher. Everyone wanted to fight me, even kids from the local middle schools and high schools. I lived five miles out of town in the country and had to learn to defend myself quickly. It did not matter what my age was, my size was what the other kids saw. So taking up Judo at the local YMCA was the start of my first martial arts education, and I also took up wrestling in my elementary school.

Over the years I studied many other styles as well. I have always searched for ways to improve my knowledge of martial arts. One day I was sharing kata with a work associate. He showed me a pressure point technique using Stomach-10. I was hooked and needed to learn more. I hit the internet and started doing some research and found Grandmaster Dillman. I immediately called him up and ordered all of his books and video tapes. Eventually he came to Florida for a seminar and I took one of my students and we attended his special pressure point training classes. I was quickly applying my book knowledge to firsthand experience.

We all know what it is like trying to learn martial arts. Every time you move, you end up having to learn another style of martial arts because there is nothing in the local area for the other styles you have studied. Well, I decided to change my strategy. I always wanted to move home to my birthplace of Hershey, Pennsylvania. It just so happened that Grandmaster Dillman lives an hour or two away in Reading, Pennsylvania. So I packed up the family and we moved home.

As soon as I moved to Hershey, I called George and asked if I could meet up with him. We met at a nearby restaurant in Lebanon to have dinner together. While sitting at the dinner table George tested my knowledge a bit and even struck me in Gall Bladder 20 while I was sitting in my chair. But then he asked if I had seen some of his new special techniques. I always want to learn more, so I stood up in between tables in the restaurant. Next thing I knew... Bang! I was down on the floor wondering what just happened. He knocked me out in the restaurant filled with people sitting all around us. As I stood up there was a huge smile across my face. A new relationship had just begun, one of Grandmaster and his new loyal student.

Ryūkyū Kempo

◆ **DAVID RHODES, INDIANA, USA** ◆

In the late 80s, I hosted a Dillman seminar in Indianapolis. The seminar site was a room in a recreational sports facility on a college campus that had windows facing an interior hallway as well as windows to the outside. The seminar was attended by many high level black belts, a few lower ranks, and also members of a police SWAT team.

Master Dillman spoke briefly about pressure points and martial arts and then picked a student to demonstrate on. His technique was a chop to the arm and a tap to the side of the neck—what had always been explained as a "block" in kata. I knew what to expect from my previous seminar experiences: after the tap to the neck the student would explain that he was dizzy and how it felt like the energy from the tap went up over his head to the other side of his face. A great technique to explain to everyone that a "block" was not a block.

But this time the student collapsed.

At the time I just thought his pressure points must have been more sensitive (it was not until after the seminar that Master Dillman found out that the student used illegal drugs and had in fact used them the night before the seminar). Master Dillman began his revival but the student stayed "out." It took a while, with Master Dillman performing almost three complete revival cycles, before the student started coming to his senses. Even then he was listless and could not stand up or walk very well without assistance. Master Dillman asked that someone take him outside and walk him around to get him feeling better and then he continued with the seminar.

You would think everyone's attention would now be on Master Dillman. After all, he had just shown everyone what a "block" from a kata could actually do. He was getting ready to show them what their kata actually meant. But there was one slight problem. The person walking the student around had decided to walk him in the hallway just outside the classroom, where everyone could see them through the *inside* windows. So no-one was paying any attention to Master Dillman; they were only watching the person as he stumbled and swayed while being walked back and forth past the classroom windows.

Master Dillman stopped for a moment and went into the hallway and asked that the person be taken outside for some fresh air. He was taken outside, and of course, walked back and forth past the *outside* windows! Once again, everyone was watching this instead of paying attention to Master Dillman!

The seminar was completed and everyone learned a lot of information. I know because I spoke with several of the black belts who had attended. But of course what they remembered most was the student going out and then being paraded past the windows!

◆ Dusty Seale, Illinois, USA ◆

I first met George Dillman at a seminar in the Chicago area in 1988. I had already been training in martial arts for twelve years. I instantly saw something different at this seminar. Everything made sense and worked much better than the traditional explanations I had been told. This all became amazingly clear at the end of the seminar. Dillman brought a man up and was in the process of demonstrating a higher meaning of the traditional "shuto block" you find in kata. I was sitting only a few feet away to witness this demonstration.

Master Dillman was grabbing the man's right wrist with his left hand on two pressure points that I later learned affected the heart and the lungs. Master Dillman held those points while he started to explain to the crowd what they did and what he was about to do. While Master Dillman was talking, the man fell face first onto the gym floor. His head was directly in front of me and he was not moving! Master Dillman reached down to pull the man back to his feet. As he did, blood started to flow on the gym floor from the man slamming his face on it! Master Dillman was visibly shaken and yanked the man up and started working on reviving him. The man's face was gray and he was not breathing!

Dillman eventually brought the man back and took a break to gather himself. I later found out from my instructor, Bob "Pitbull" Golden, that the man admitted to snorting cocaine before the seminar. Since cocaine has an effect on the heart and lungs, his body shut down because Dillman was using pressure points which affect those organs. At the end of the seminar Master Dillman explained to the seminar what had happened and that the man's heart and lungs stopped working briefly and that is why he was gray! Master Dillman then also taught us how to restart the heart, head, and lungs. I knew right then and there this was the answer to martial arts!

◆ ◆ ◆ ◆ ◆

In the mid-90s we were at a seminar in Chicago. After the seminar there was a very large man who flew in from California to attend the seminar. This man was, if I remember correctly, a third degree black belt in a jujitsu style under one of the biggest names in jujitsu. The man was talking to the host of the seminar and explaining how he could take him down, and then proceeded to take the host to the ground and lock him up. Master Dillman was signing autographs and taking photos while all of this was going on, but he saw the whole thing.

One thing about Dillman is that he is incredibly smart and doesn't miss anything. So the jujitsuka came over to Master Dillman and said very proudly, "Did you see that sensei?" Looking back on it and now knowing the jujitsuka, I do not believe he was challenging Dillman, but at the time it came across that way. Master Dillman stood up from his table and said, "Yeah I saw that but you can't do that to me." The jujitsuka believed he could and Dillman told him to try.

The jujitsuka said, "Get in your fighting stance." Dillman was standing with toes pointed straight forward, feet shoulder width apart and replied, "I'm in it." Dillman came up to roughly the man's chest area. The jujitsuka shot in to take Dillman down. Dillman did a movement from the end of kata Seisan, clipping the jujitsuka on a pressure point on the back of his head and one on his face, then threw the man into the wall by his head (that move is also in the kata by the way)!

Bob Golden and I looked at each other in shock. Dillman then picked the man up and revived him from being knocked out and invited him to dinner with us! The man has been part of Dillman's organization ever since.

◆ **KEN SMITH, ILLINOIS, USA** ◆

In 2007, I was invited by my good friend and teacher, George Dillman, to teach a session during his three-day seminar, in London, England. Shortly after my session started, I pulled up a willing participant to demonstrate a technique. Using one of my favorite moves, I struck him with a hit to Stomach 5. This uke, a 6'3", 250 pound man, hit the floor so hard and suddenly that the weight of his body falling almost pulled me on top of him.

George, who didn't know that I could do knockouts, and had never witnessed me doing one, leapt to his feet and rushed to the teaching floor. "Get him up! Get him up," George told me in a nervous, yet proud tone. He watched me revive the man and was satisfied with my technique. As he walked back to his place in the crowd, he looked over his shoulder and told the crowd, "See, even my stick guy can do knock outs!" Everyone laughed, and that was my first public knock out.

Ryūkyū Kempo

◆ STEVE STEWART, CANADA ◆

Since meeting Grandmaster Dillman in 1989, he has taken me under his wing and encouraged me to expand my knowledge of Kyusho. Back in March of 2000 I hosted a seminar for him in London, Ontario, Canada, and we had over 250 people in attendance. I have a 5000 square foot dojo but we needed more room! I had half a dozen buses show up and we transported everyone to a nearby school to use their gym.

There was also a huge snowstorm, but people still came out to see Grandmaster Dillman! He has welcomed me as an instructor at his training camps and allowed me to act as his representative. He has also inspired me to go back to college and get my doctorate in Traditional Chinese Medicine. Words cannot describe how indebted I am to him for supporting me and my family over the years.

◆ LANCE STRONG, NEW ZEALAND ◆

I first met George Dillman in New Zealand in 1988 when he was touring with Professor Wally Jay. At one of Wally Jay's seminars, I was introduced to George and he said he could knock out people by hitting them on the arm using pressure points. Needing to be a believer I stuck my arm out and George knocked me out. After that I was a believer. From that point on I attended as many of George's seminars in New Zealand as possible.

In 1990, we took a New Zealand Team to George's Northeast Championships and I had the privilege of staying with George and learning so much more. Since 1990 my wife Ava and I have lived in the USA for four years, and have also travelled many times from New Zealand to train with Grandmaster Dillman. On many occasions we stayed with George and Kim Dillman. We've also travelled with them in their motor home and on seminar tours to Cleveland, Detroit, and Chicago, where we learned so much and made lifelong friends with many of the fine people in the DKI organization.

The martial arts world owes George Dillman a huge debt of gratitude for the pioneering manner in which he brought the knowledge of kata and pressure points back into mainstream martial arts. This knowledge has rejuvenated and stimulated many martial arts organizations throughout the world, and for this, and for his charismatic and fantastic sense of humor, I am proud to acknowledge Grandmaster Dillman as an amazing martial arts mentor and friend, and as a global martial arts pioneer.

◆ Ava Strong, New Zealand ◆

The main thing I remember is the fun my husband Lance and I had with George and Kim traveling throughout the USA. A tour in George's bus consisted of many stops to sing karaoke and to run "packed house" seminars on pressure point applications. Students would be falling left right and center, with dumbfounded looks on their faces and stars in their eyes. Luckily the catchers would stop them from harming themselves as they got knockout and then revived, most still shaking their heads in disbelief, now true believers in the Dillman Pressure Point method.

George was always entertaining in his way of teaching and always ready for a laugh. I remember a seminar in Detroit City where Dan Severn and his training partner Eric attended. Eric had a bright red gi top which George could pick out very easily. Every time George needed to demonstrate, he pulled Eric out, right up until lunch break. So Eric was getting to feel all the points in his body over and over again! After the break we started again and George went to demonstrate and looked around and couldn't see the red gi and so chose another student. What had happened was Eric had realized the red top was not a good idea, and put a black gi on during the break, so now he wasn't so obvious! We all had a good laugh with George about this after the seminar. I'd like to take the opportunity to say thanks George for the fun times and wonderful memories, but most of all for his great contribution to the martial arts world.

Ryūkyū Kempo

♦ DR. CHARLES TERRY, PENNSYLVANIA ♦

I have been a student of George Dillman since 1979. After earning a Black Belt in Tang Soo Do, I discovered the art of Okinawan Kempo when one of Dillman's students opened a school near my house. The well-rounded curriculum was quite appealing even before the emphasis on pressure point techniques. Dillman had quite a reputation with tournament competition. He freely shared his expertise in weapons, kata, sparring, breaking, and ground fighting through seminars at our school several times per year. For a time he held the world record for breaking the most ice with his elbow. I loved reading articles about him and watching him on TV shows such as *Real People*. I got to see his ice break live as well as his sword demonstration. He could cut a watermelon with a sword on someone's bare stomach while blindfolded without injuring the volunteer!

Back then, training was pretty hard core. Having started over as a white belt in Okinawan Kempo, I had the honor of testing under Grandmaster Dillman for Brown Belt. While we were doing kata *Sanchin*, he tested our focus by breaking boards on our heads and hitting and kicking us. I'll never forget how the whole line of students was moved back several feet after he drilled each student in the stomach with a front kick!

Things really became exciting in the early 1980s when Grandmaster Dillman began an affiliation with Seiyu Oyata. The seminars jointly taught by Dillman and Oyata were incredible. Kata and techniques we had practiced for years suddenly took on new life with the added component of pressure points. In 1986, I founded the University of Pennsylvania Ryukyu

Kempo Club as an affiliate of Dillman Karate International. I had an interest in acupuncture, but felt it was an awful lot of material to learn for what might be just the placebo effect. This changed when I saw how effective pressure points were in self-defense. I realized that if they worked in self-defense, perhaps acupuncture points would also be effective in healing.

Grandmaster Dillman encouraged my interest in medical school and in studying acupuncture after I completed my residency in Physiatry (Physical Medicine and Rehabilitation). I scheduled as many rotations as I could near his home dojo in Reading, Pennsylvania. He knew I was just a poor student at the time. Not only did he graciously allow me to train with him free of charge, but he often took me out to dinner afterwards. He introduced me to Professor Presas and Professor Jay. I was honored to host "Triple Seminars" in the Philadelphia area from 1994 until the death of Professor Presas and the retirement of Wally Jay. After this, we continued with "Double Impact" Seminars featuring Grandmaster Dillman and Professor Leon Jay for many years.

He was also responsible for my affiliation with Grandmaster Leo Fong. I will be forever grateful for his openness to other systems and styles. It is often said, "There is more than one way to reach the top of the mountain." Being able to study the arts of Modern Arnis, Small Circle Jujitsu, and Wei Kuen Do in conjunction with Ryukyu Kempo has certainly made the path more interesting.

George Dillman has been supportive during every phase of my martial arts career. In 1997, I opened MKA Karate. Grandmaster Dillman has been a special guest on many occasions. We proudly follow curriculum based on his color belt and black belt requirements from the 1970s and 1980s with innovations that connect the modern era with classical Ryukyu Kempo.

Because of his in-depth and never-ending study of pressure points and theory, as well as sharing with the arts of Professor Presas, Professor Jay, and Professor Fong, we will never be at a loss for new material. This spirit of camaraderie extends to all of the members of Dillman's organization. At his prompting, and by his example, his Black Belts continue to develop new techniques and theories. By working together, this approach contributes to furthering everyone's growth, and continues to push the martial arts world (often kicking and screaming) into the future.

Ryūkyū Kempo

◆ CHRIS THOMAS, WISCONSIN, USA ◆

I will always remember my first meeting with Sensei Dillman. He himself loves to tell the story of that first meeting. I went to a Dillman seminar with a *kohai* (junior). A local TV news crew was there, so they taped a little of the demonstration. Sensei grabbed my *kohai* (I was there to serve as catcher—a great intro to pressure points for me) and tapped him on Triple Warmer 17 (*Yifeng*). As he collapsed, his legs kicked apart, spreading two sections of the portable stage we were on, and he fell into the space. The news cameraman was using a medium shot from the waist up, so on TV it looked as though *kohai* simply vanished!

Later that evening, outside a Chinese restaurant Sensei introduced me to Gall Bladder 20 (*Fengchi*). I went home feeling like a white belt. I kept thinking about the Zen concept of 'beginner's mind,' and about how long it had been since I had felt this way, and I was delighted. And while I don't feel like a white belt anymore, my usual reaction to training with Sensei is: "Can I give rank back?"

◆ JERRY VEGA, PENNSYLVANIA, USA ◆

There is a karate master in our midst, and although many would like to meet him and ask him questions, some are afraid or unable to believe in the knowledge and message this man has to share. Several months ago, this master walked into a local barbershop for his regular haircut. While sitting quietly and talking to the other patrons, a young man, almost twice the master's size, walked into the shop. This young man was quickly noticed because of his approach (loud and demanding attention). The young man noticed the master sitting in the barber's chair and immediately approached with a challenge.

"Karate is useless," he said. "What you need are these," and with that the young man exposed and flexed his biceps muscle. The young man continued to challenge the art of karate and the master's ability. The master recalled his own youth, the many challengers he had faced throughout his life, and held back his temper. He simply invited the young man to touch him. At that, the young man made his approach and attempted to grab the older man. A moment later the master was helping the young man up from the floor. The young man could not understand what had just occurred, and began to question and express doubt. Once again the master found himself helping the young man from the floor.

The young man asked the master if he was trying to make a fool of him. The master answered, "No sir, you did that the moment you walked in the door and opened your mouth." The lesson I learned from this encounter was: When angry hold back your hand; when you must strike out with your hand, hold back your anger.

◆ MICKEY WITTEKIEND, ILLINOIS, USA ◆

Mr. Dillman has done more for me than anyone in karate. Because of his knowledge and teaching, my wife, Teri, and I have run a successful martial arts school for twenty years. Armed with the pressure point knowledge taught to me by George Dillman, my fellow martial artists, Chris Thomas, Dusty Seal, and I taught the US Marine Corps and helped start the Marine Corps' martial arts program that is still being taught today.

George Dillman is, in my opinion, one of the greatest martial artist alive. What most people don't know is he is also one of the funniest men around as well. His stories of his travels are hilarious. He is also one the kindest, most caring men you could have for a friend.

Ryūkyū Kempo

◆ DANIEL YOUNG, PENNSYLVANIA, USA ◆

I remember the first time I met George Dillman. I thought, "They say he's good, but will his technique work on me?" Needless to say after asking to be his *uke* once, it did! He would just touch me and I'd jolt! He's like a fire ant: He looks like your normal person, but he will sting you, and deep down when he does! George has an energy that lights up a room.

He is as playful with people as he is passionate about the martial arts. I always have to warn my students that when they first meet him, he likes to shake their hand and then use his other hand to tap on the large intestine meridian on their arm so that he can set them up for a knockout. He doesn't want to leave any skeptics behind. Trust me, none of my students are!

A few years ago, we were posing for pictures at the Muhammad Ali Training Camp, and while two of my students were kneeling on one knee in front of George, he used his big toes to step on the Kidney One pressure points on the bottom of their feet. They instantly felt the effects, as shown on their faces in the photo. They still laugh about that to this day. This is just George being George. He has an incredibly playful personality!

The legacy that George has built is not only for the work that he has done to research the pressure points and show the world what their arts are missing, but also the organization that he has created. No-one can dispute that George has built a solid group of people who are not only loyal to George, but also to each other. You will not find a friendlier group of people anywhere. Their love for the martial arts shows not only in their technique, but also in their desire to help others be the best that they can be. This can all be traced back to the foundation that was created by George Dillman.

CHAPTER TWENTY-EIGHT:
The Act of Succession

> Seventy-five years is quite a mile-marker. It is three-quarters of a century. In social science, it is coming up on two-and-a-half generations. For anniversaries, it is commemorated by diamonds. It terms of the journey of life, it certainly provides a good-deal of perspective with which to consider the path so far.
>
> On a dark and stormy night in July 2017, the Dillmans hosted just such a retrospective, fueled by perhaps the best lasagna in North America and beer brewed using the cleanest water in all the world! The wheels of the old analogue tape recorder whirred late into the evening, while the rumble of thunder and insistent hammering of the rain on glass outside this warm bubble of hospitality underscored the messages that were being delivered…

- **On his teachers:** I've had a lot of teachers over the years, and learned something from each of them. Oyata used to say: "If I asked, 'Who was your teacher in high school,' you wouldn't give just one name." You pick up different things from different teachers. I have had many teachers over the years.

I did have a special connection with Hohan Soken though, even if it was brief. In 1972 he started to show me the real meaning of kata. It hurt him that people all over the United States didn't understand it, and he asked me how we could get this knowledge out. I didn't know it at the time, but the availability of video cameras in the 1970s, training with Seiyu Oyata in the 1980s, and publishing books with Chris Thomas in the 1990s turned out to be the way.

Ryūkyū Kempo

Many years later I was teaching a class at a local gym, and a man who was clearly an experienced martial artist stopped by. After the class was over, we got talking. He was visiting the U.S. from South America. He said, "I have seen a lot of people doing beautiful kata during my visit." When I told him that many of them probably did not know the meaning of the moves they were doing, he was amazed. He didn't understand how that could be. And then I found out that he had been a student of Hohan Soken (*Ed. In 1924, Soken emigrated to Argentina, where he taught karate for many years before returning to Japan in 1952*).

♦ **On his students:** I've seen a lot of students come and go over the years. Some—like Chas Terry and Ralph Buschbaker—trained with me since they were kids. Others started with different teachers, in other systems, and 'adopted' me over the years. Some have left, sometimes on good terms, and sometimes on bad terms. Some have even stolen from me. One group tried to put the Hohan Soken notes on the internet, but they only had the questions [*the location of the points*], not the answers [*how to hit and what effect it would cause*]. Angle and direction is still the most important part of pressure point technique. Another put the forms reserved for high-level black belts on video and sold it. But whenever someone who just took from me teaches my system somewhere in the world, I get a ton of book orders from there right afterwards! And through the years, the good ones have remained—I am so proud of them...

♦ **On his colleagues:** I miss Remy [Presas] every day. We used to have so much fun on the road together. He loved my camper-van, and used to ask me, "How many seminars I have to do to buy one?" I'd guess fifty to sixty, and he'd say, "So many!?" I miss Wally Jay as well. From the minute we got together, we shared techniques from our systems. At first, his students didn't believe pressure points worked, but I made a believer out of Wally, and he made believers out of them! Leo Fong and I still chat all the time. He's in such great shape. Maybe it's all the kale he eats! I do the same thing. Anyone would be lucky to be in that shape at his age.

♦ **On the early days:** I wouldn't change a thing. Even though I trained for many years before discovering pressure points, it gave me the delivery system for pressure point striking. It also taught me how to teach and put together an organization. The military did a lot for me as well. That training, and my early martial arts, gave me the confidence to walk into hundreds of dojos, alone—no right hand man—surrounded by champions, street fighters, and grapplers—sometimes as many as sixty, who thought they could take me—and make believers out of them all. And once the seminar was over, it was *over*. No hard feelings. No "what ifs." No grudges. In all that time, no-one was ever seriously injured. That's not bad.

♦ **On his method:** I was known for letting my students demonstrate their abilities at the end of my seminars. A lot of people thought that this was just to let them shine—and it was—but there were other reasons as well. For one thing, it showed everybody that I wasn't the only one who could make these techniques work. And for another, it's a great motivator to make students practice to perfect their techniques!

♦ **On the future:** I am pretty much retired now. No more seminars. I have an amazing group of senior instructors all over the world, and my hope for the future is that they will work together and support each other. Because my art can be used in a variety of systems, some people focus on one part of the method, and others focus on another. Between them all, they have the whole system. I don't think I am done making promotions, but I have very strict standards for the highest ranks.

If I could choose one piece of advice for future generations of instructors to put on the dojo wall, it would be this:

Give your students your time, your energy, and your love.
They will show if you are the real thing...

Ryūkyū Kempo

EPILOGUE:
Prometheus

According to Greek legend, Prometheus was the son of a Titan—a race of immortals who ruled the ancient world for a time until they were overthrown by a new generation of deities known as "the Olympians." He was also fearless. Undaunted by the supposed omnipotence of Zeus, he set out to prove the new ruler fallible by offering him two sacrifices, one of which had a pleasing exterior but was worthless within, and the other of which appeared on its face to be much less appealing, but concealed a far more wholesome content.

Zeus fell for the trick, and in his anger at having been fooled in this manner, confiscated the secret of fire from man. Prometheus, however, stole it back from the gods and returned it to the world so that all people might once again share in this powerful knowledge. For this deed humankind was eternally grateful, but Zeus punished Prometheus by chaining him to a large stone where a great eagle would swoop down every day to devour his liver.

Prometheus was eventually freed by the hero Hercules, and went on to warn Zeus of a great threat to his life, thereby reconciling these two mythic figures. Opinions differ as to whether Prometheus should be hailed for his bravery and cunning, or despised for his transgression against the Olympians, but one thing is clear: he played a pivotal role in the development of human knowledge, bringing light to a place where there was once only darkness...

> No one person, organization, or culture can lay claim to such knowledge—it belongs to all humankind.
>
> —The Master

Ryūkyū Kempo

THE AUTHORS:
Kubichiridushi

As the perceptive reader will have detected, *Kubichiridushi* is not a person; rather, it is a peculiarly Okinawan expression meaning "fast friends" or "blood brothers" (or even, as Mark Marshall so humorously explains in his piece, "best buddies").

Because this work represents the collaborative efforts of many such friends, it is appropriate that authorship be credited this way. It also speaks to the strength of the ties that bind Ryūkyū Kempo practitioners the world over together in their love of this art, and their dedication to this way.

www.ingramcontent.com/pod-product-compliance
Lightning Source LLC
Chambersburg PA
CBHW051052160426
43193CB00010B/1155